Getting Started with OpenGL ES 3+ Programming

Hans de Ruiter

Version 1.6 – 2024 – Updated the cover
Version 1.5 – 2023 – Added SDL_HINT_OPENGL_ES_DRIVER to OpenGL (ES 3.x) init code
Version 1.4 – 2023 – updated for newer Visual Studio versions
Version 1.3 – 2019 – updated for print
Version 1.2 – 2019 – updated for ebook file formats
Version 1.1 – 2017

Distribute the Link, Not the Book
It takes a lot of time and effort to produce resources like this, and we think it's great when people find it useful and want to share. However, please share the following link instead of distributing (illegal) copies. That way they get a legitimate copy and we're able to continue producing quality content:
https://keasigmadelta.com/gles3-sdl2-tutorial

We've done everything we can to make the contents of this book as accurate as possible. However, due to the complex nature of the topics and possible human error, we cannot guarantee absolute accuracy. Also, continual research and development means that things are ever changing. No liability is assumed for losses or damages due to the information provided. You are responsible for your own choices, actions, and results.

Table of Contents

Introduction

Welcome to this tutorial series, and congratulations for taking this first step. Maybe you're interested in creating a game from scratch, and/or want to understand the code. Maybe you're dreaming of writing your own game engine, or becoming a developer at a game studio. Or maybe you want to learn graphics programming for some other reason entirely. Whatever the case, you're here.

These tutorials will give you an accelerated path from zero through to rendering stuff in 3D. You will learn modern OpenGL that's usable on both desktop and mobile devices. No, it won't get you to AAA game engine level as that's a huge task. However, it will give you the fundamentals you need before you can build more complicated stuff.

IMPORTANT: If your sole goal is to write a computer game and you don't care about the code, then you may wish to look for a ready-made game engine instead. There are many game engines out there that can get your project underway faster. These tutorials are for those who want to learn how to do graphics programming which will help you build custom graphics engines or tailor existing ones to your needs.

Who is this For?

These tutorials are intended for people with almost zero OpenGL programming experience. Having some C/C++ coding experience is helpful, but not required. The tutorials will explain the code at a fairly basic level.

That said, if you have no programming experience, then I recommend learning the basics of programming in C as well (e.g., follow this free online course: http://www.learn-c.org/).

Why OpenGL ES 3+ and SDL2?

There are a mind-boggling array of options out there: OpenGL, Direct-X, Vulkan, Metal, GLUT, GLFW, etc. Which is best? How to choose?

I've chosen to teach OpenGL ES 3+ (GLES3) because it's modern and available on all major mobile devices and is usable on desktops too. This maximises your options. Systems like Direct-X and Metal are restricted to specific platforms, and Vulkan is very complicated to use (definitely not good for beginners).

SDL2 (or Simple Direct-media Layer 2) takes care of low-level stuff like opening windows/screens, handling user input from joysticks, keyboards, touch, etc.. These tasks are normally platform dependent, and SDL2 gives you a common way of using them. There are other options like GLFW and GLUT, but I prefer SDL2. It has good support for both desktop and mobile devices, and provides a wide range of features, including multi-touch support, image loading (via SDL_image), etc. SDL2 also provides access to OS native objects should you want to use platform-specific features.

Don't worry about whether SDL2 really is the best choice for you because it can always be replaced later if you wish. The key right now is to get started.

How to Get the Most Out of These Tutorials

Simply owning a copy of these tutorials won't magically give you expertise. It takes work, or to put it another way: "you still have to do your own push-ups." Here are a few tips on how to get the most out of these tutorials.

First, follow the tutorials step-by-step. They've been written in a specific order for a reason; it's what works best.

Write code by hand. It's very tempting to copy and paste the code from this book to save time. Resist that urge, because you'll learn and remember more by typing out the code manually.

Next, try to go through the tutorials on a regular schedule, e.g., one per day or maybe one every few days. You'll learn and remember more with regular practise then trying to cram everything in a few sessions (e.g., 1 hour a day beats 7 hour marathons once a week)

Third, do the exercises and perform your own experiments. Try changing the code to do something else, e.g., draw a square instead of a triangle, change the texture or the colour, etc.

Finally, I've written a "Modern Graphics Programming Primer" to accompany these tutorials. While the tutorials teach you *how* to code graphics, you'll be more capable if you understand *what* the hardware is doing (at least at a high level). The primer covers things such as: how modern GPUs work, 3D coordinate systems, and the underlying theory.

You can get the primer at: https://keasigmadelta.com/graphics-primer

What if I Get Stuck?

There's a lot to learn, and you're likely to get stuck at some point. Here's what to do:

1. Try to figure it out yourself first

2. If you're still stuck, search the internet for a solution. Chances are high that someone else has experienced your problem already, and published a solution

3. Ask for help. Send me a message (https://keasigmadelta.com/support/)

Follow this process; resist the urge to jump to step 3 immediately. This isn't for purely selfish reasons (I can't respond to huge numbers of queries); it's also better for you. By following this process you're training yourself for developing software the real world. It's how professional software developers solve problems.

That said, don't be afraid to reach out for help if you need it. I'm happy to help, and knowing what people get stuck on will help me improve these tutorials.

Tutorial 1: Getting Started

This tutorial we'll be setting up our development environment, and creating a basic GLES3 app. It won't do much; just open a window and clear it to black. The goal is simply to get something basic working.

Setting Up the Development Environment

To write GLES3 + SDL2 apps we need a suitable development environment (dev-environment) that allows us to write code and compile it. There are two parts to this. First, we need to install the code editor and compiler. Second, most dev-environments don't come with GLES3 and SDL2 support out of the box. Their dev-files need to be installed before we can use them.

NOTE: This tutorial currently only covers using Visual Studio on Windows. Don't worry about developing for mobile devices yet; just get the basics working on your desktop computers. If you're using MacOS X or some other platform then search the internet for how you set up a compiler (e.g., here's one for SDL2 on MacOS X: http://lazyfoo.net/tutorials/SDL/01_hello_SDL/mac/index.php).

Setup on Windows

Microsoft provide a comprehensive dev-environment called Visual Studio. So download that now from: https://www.visualstudio.com/downloads/

IMPORTANT: Download the free *Visual Studio Community* edition. The free version provides all that you need.

Start the Visual Studio installer, and select the "Custom," (Figure 1).

Figure 1: Choose the custom installation type.

Click the "Next" button. Next, make sure that you're installing Visual C++ (see Figure 2).

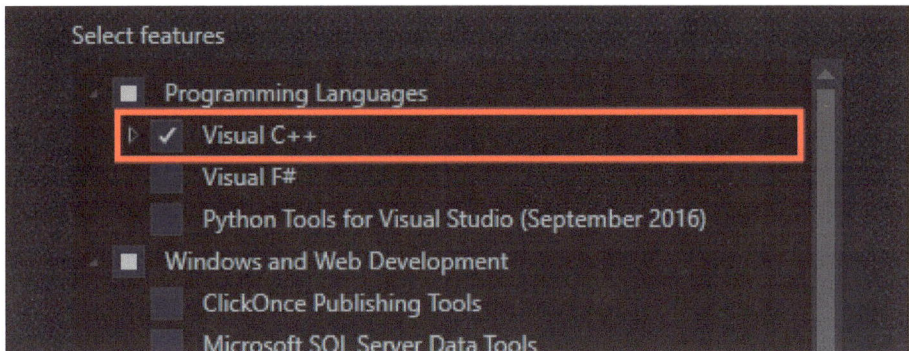

Figure 2: Select the features to install.

With this done, click "Next," then "Install," and wait for the installer to complete.

Installing the GLES3 & SDL2 Development Files

On Windows you need two sets of dev-files:

- Angle (for GLES3 support) - https://github.com/google/angle

- SDL2 - https://www.libsdl.org/download-2.0.php

The setup process is currently rather tedious, so I've created a template that does it all for you. Download the template from: https://keasigmadelta.com/assets/GLTutorials/GLES3SDL2-Application.zip

To install the template, copy the downloaded file to: "<My Documents folder>\Visual Studio <year>\Templates\ProjectTemplates\Visual C++ Project", where <My Documents folder> is the path to your documents folder, and <year> is your Visual Studio's year number (e.g., 2023, if you have Visual Studio 2023). See Figure 3 for an example.

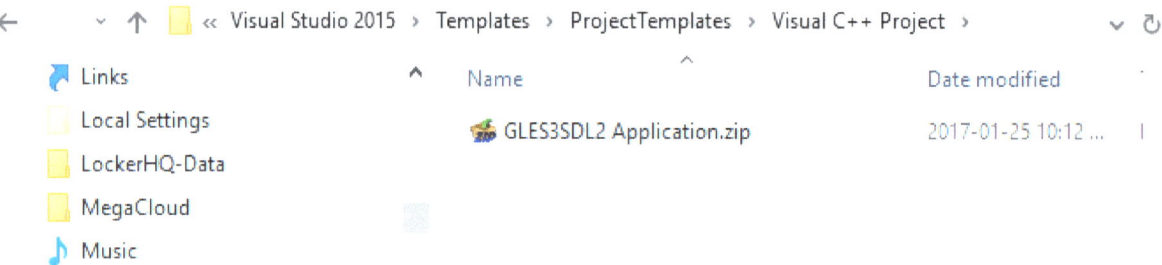

Figure 3: The template is installed by copying it to the project templates folder.

Create a New Project

Now we can create our project. In Visual Studio, select File => New => Project from the menu. Select the "GLES3SDL2 Application" template, and call the project something like "GLTutorial1" (Figure 4). After clicking "OK" it'll create the new project.

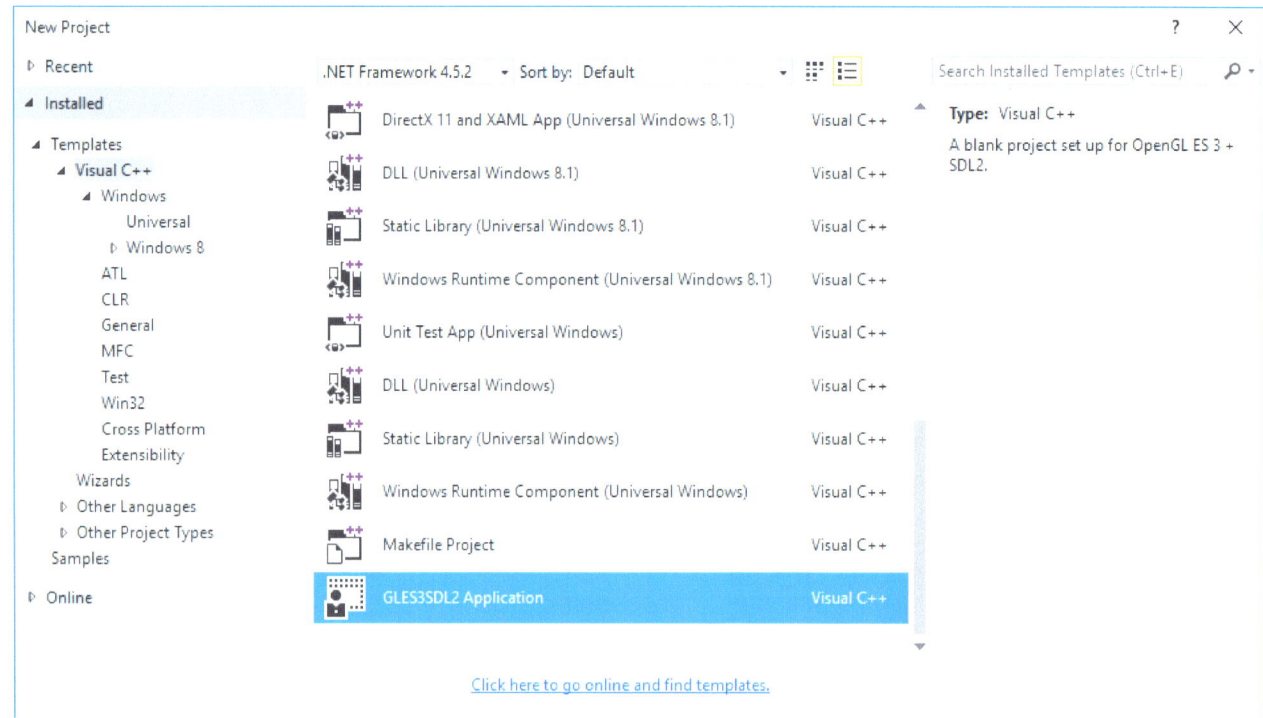

Figure 4: Create a new project using the GLES2SDL2 Application template.

Next, right-click on the new "GLTutorial1" project in the Solution Explorer (on the left) and select build. With the first build it'll set up SDL2 and Angle within the project. The Angle files are in a self-extracting archive. It'll pop up a window asking you where to put it (Figure 5). Simply click the Extract button.

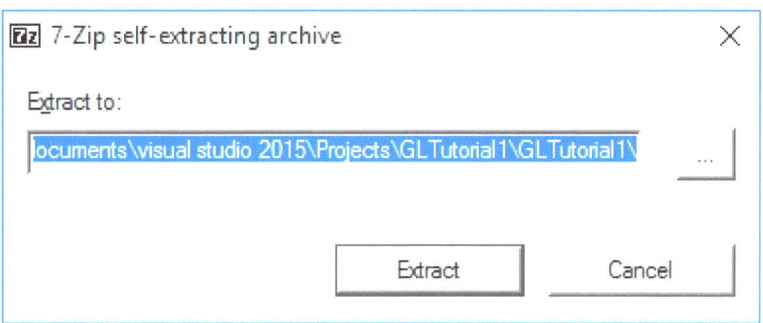

Figure 5: Click Extract to unpack the Angle files.

NOTE: Visual Studio's editor may claim it can't find "SDL.h" despite having installed the SDL2 package during the initial build. Simply close and reopen the project/solution (File => Close Solution, followed by File => Recent Projects and Solutions => GLTutorial1.sln).

Our First GLES3 & SDL2 Program

Right! Let's get into actual coding, and write our first GLES3 + SDL program. In the solution explorer (left column), open Main.cpp. You'll find it under GLTutorial1 => Source Files. Delete the existing code, and start writing.

IMPORTANT: As mentioned in the How to Get the Most Out of These Tutorials section (on page 6), it's highly recommended that you type out the code by hand instead of copying and pasting. You'll learn/remember more if you do it that way.

Headers and Definitions

We'll start by including the header files for libraries we're using (SDL2 & OpenGL). Here's the code:

```
// Basic OpenGL ES 3 + SDL2 template code

#include <SDL.h>
```

```
#include <SDL_opengles2.h>
#include <GLES3/gl3.h>
#include <cstdio>
#include <cstdlib>
```

Next, comes a few constants for the window's dimensions:

```
const unsigned int DISP_WIDTH = 640;
const unsigned int DISP_HEIGHT = 480;
```

SDL and OpenGL Initialization

Its time to set up SDL and create a window with an OpenGL ES 3 context. This is the start of your program. With SDL, the main entry point is *SDL_main()*. This is optional, but worth using because it hides the difference between main() & WinMain() (or whatever special main entry point an OS may have). Anyway, SDL is initialized as follows (put this directly below the headers and definitions):

```
int SDL_main(int argc, char *args[]) {
    // The window
    SDL_Window *window = NULL;

    // The OpenGL context
    SDL_GLContext context = NULL;

    // Init SDL
    if (SDL_Init(SDL_INIT_VIDEO) < 0) {
        SDL_Log("SDL could not initialize! SDL_Error: %s\n", SDL_GetError());
        return EXIT_FAILURE;
    }

    // Setup the exit hook
    atexit(SDL_Quit);
```

Notice that we're only initializing SDL's video subsystem in the SDL_Init() call:

```
    if (SDL_Init(SDL_INIT_VIDEO) < 0) {
```

SDL has other sub-systems such as audio and joystick input, but we're not using any of them.

Next, we request OpenGL ES 3.0, and double-buffering:

```c
// Request OpenGL ES 3.0
SDL_GL_SetAttribute(SDL_GL_CONTEXT_PROFILE_MASK,
        );
SDL_GL_SetAttribute(SDL_GL_CONTEXT_MAJOR_VERSION, 3);
SDL_GL_SetAttribute(SDL_GL_CONTEXT_MINOR_VERSION, 0);

// Force usage of the GLES backend
SDL_SetHint(SDL_HINT_OPENGL_ES_DRIVER, "1");

// Want double-buffering
SDL_GL_SetAttribute(SDL_GL_DOUBLEBUFFER, 1);
```

Double-buffering is a technique whereby we render to an invisible back-buffer and then flip the buffers round to show it. Rendering directly to the screen runs the risk that partially rendered images are shown. We definitely don't want that because it's ugly.

Opening the Window

With base initialization done, we can now open the window and set up the OpenGL context:

```c
// Create the window
window = SDL_CreateWindow("GLES3+SDL2 Tutorial", SDL_WINDOWPOS_UNDEFINED,
    SDL_WINDOWPOS_UNDEFINED, DISP_WIDTH, DISP_HEIGHT,
    SDL_WINDOW_OPENGL | SDL_WINDOW_SHOWN);
if (!window) {
    SDL_ShowSimpleMessageBox(SDL_MESSAGEBOX_ERROR, "Error",
    "Couldn't create the main window.", NULL);
    return EXIT_FAILURE;
}

context = SDL_GL_CreateContext(window);
if (!context) {
    SDL_ShowSimpleMessageBox(SDL_MESSAGEBOX_ERROR, "Error",
    "Couldn't create an OpenGL context.", NULL);
    return EXIT_FAILURE;
}
```

The code above has two steps; create the window (*SDL_CreateWindow()*), and create the OpenGL context (*SDL_GL_CreateContext()*). Everything else is error handling. If you wish to use OpenGL then it's very important to pass SDL_CreateWindow() the **SDL_WINDOW_OPENGL** flag. Otherwise the SDL_GL_CreateContext() call will fail.

Draw Something

Yes, it's finally time to draw something! Okay, all we're going to do this tutorial is clear the screen, but it'll still be an OpenGL draw operation nonetheless. Clearing to black is done as follows:

```
// Clear to black
glClearColor(0.0f, 0.0f, 0.0f, 1.0f);
glClear(GL_COLOR_BUFFER_BIT);

// Update the window
SDL_GL_SwapWindow(window);
```

GL_COLOR_BUFFER_BIT tells *glClear()* to only clear the screen/image (a.k.a., colour buffer). A context may also have depth/z and stencil buffers, and you may wish to clear one or more of them. The clear colour is, unsurprisingly, set by *glClearColor()*. Finally, *SDL_GL_SwapWindow()* swaps the buffers so that our new image is displayed. We enabled double-buffering (by passing *SDL_GL_DOUBLEBUFFER* to *SDL_GL_SetAttribute()*) so rendering is performed on an invisible back buffer. So the front and back buffers need to be swapped.

Wait Until the User Wants to Quit

Normally a "real" OpenGL program would have a main loop that does things like respond to events and render animated graphics. Since this is a really basic program, all that's needed is to wait for the user to click the window's close button. SDL makes this relatively easy with its event handling functions:

```
// Wait for the user to quit
bool quit = false;
while (!quit) {
    SDL_Event event;
    if (SDL_WaitEvent(&event) != 0) {
        if (event.type == SDL_QUIT) {
            // User wants to quit
            quit = true;
```

```
                }
            }
        }

    return EXIT_SUCCESS;
}
```

SDL_WaitEvent() stops the program until an event comes in. If the incoming event is an *SDL_QUIT*, then the code above exits the while loop, and quits.

The Code in Full

Putting it all together, Main.cpp is:

```cpp
// Basic OpenGL ES 3 + SDL2 template code

#include <SDL.h>
#include <SDL_opengles2.h>
#include <GLES3/gl3.h>
#include <cstdio>
#include <cstdlib>

const unsigned int DISP_WIDTH = 640;
const unsigned int DISP_HEIGHT = 480;

int SDL_main(int argc, char *args[]) {
    // The window
    SDL_Window *window = NULL;

    // The OpenGL context
    SDL_GLContext context = NULL;

    // Init SDL
    if (SDL_Init(SDL_INIT_VIDEO) < 0) {
        fprintf(stderr, "SDL could not initialize! SDL_Error: %s\n",
SDL_GetError());
        return 10;
    }

    // Setup the exit hook
```

```
atexit(SDL_Quit);

// Request OpenGL ES 3.0
SDL_GL_SetAttribute(SDL_GL_CONTEXT_PROFILE_MASK,
    SDL_GL_CONTEXT_PROFILE_ES);
SDL_GL_SetAttribute(SDL_GL_CONTEXT_MAJOR_VERSION, 3);
SDL_GL_SetAttribute(SDL_GL_CONTEXT_MINOR_VERSION, 0);

// Force usage of the GLES backend
SDL_SetHint(SDL_HINT_OPENGL_ES_DRIVER, "1");

// Want double-buffering
SDL_GL_SetAttribute(SDL_GL_DOUBLEBUFFER, 1);


// Create the window
window = SDL_CreateWindow("GLES3+SDL2 Tutorial", SDL_WINDOWPOS_UNDEFINED,
    SDL_WINDOWPOS_UNDEFINED, DISP_WIDTH, DISP_HEIGHT,
    SDL_WINDOW_OPENGL | SDL_WINDOW_SHOWN);
if (!window) {
    SDL_ShowSimpleMessageBox(SDL_MESSAGEBOX_ERROR, "Error",
    "Couldn't create the main window.", NULL);
    return EXIT_FAILURE;
}

context = SDL_GL_CreateContext(window);
if (!context) {
    SDL_ShowSimpleMessageBox(SDL_MESSAGEBOX_ERROR, "Error",
    "Couldn't create an OpenGL context.", NULL);
    return EXIT_FAILURE;
}

// Clear to black
glClearColor(0.0f, 0.0f, 0.0f, 1.0f);
glClear(GL_COLOR_BUFFER_BIT);

// Update the window
SDL_GL_SwapWindow(window);

// Wait for the user to quit
```

```cpp
    bool quit = false;
    while (!quit) {
        SDL_Event event;
        if (SDL_WaitEvent(&event) != 0) {
            if (event.type == SDL_QUIT) {
                // User wants to quit
                quit = true;
            }
        }
    }

    return EXIT_SUCCESS;
}
```

Running the Program

Save Main.cpp, then push F5 to build and run GLTutorial1 (or right-click on the project and select Debug => Start new instance). Visual Studio will compile the program and run it. If you typed out everything correctly, you'll be greeted with the following (Figure 6).

Figure 6: GLTutorial1 running in all it's minimalist glory.

Congratulations! You just wrote your first GLES3 + SDL2 program. Yes, it's really boring, but it covers the basics you'll need to build more interesting stuff. The next tutorial covers rendering something (a single triangle).

Exercises

You've learnt the basics by example, now it's time to write some code on your own. Experimentation is a great way to learn. So, see if you can modify the code to do the following:

1. Change the window's size to 800x600

2. Change the clear colour to red, then green, blue, & yellow

Tutorial 2: Hello Triangle

This tutorial you'll finally draw something! Okay, it'll only be one triangle, but it's a big step forward. There's a lot for you to learn: namely how to use shaders and Vertex Buffer Objects (VBOs).

Most tutorial series will teach how to draw a triangle using old methods, but I don't like that idea. Those old methods are also slow and shouldn't be used in production code. There's no need to learn multiple ways to draw a triangle, so let's go straight for the method you should be using.

The Theory

Modern GPUs take large blocks of data (stored in VBOs, textures and other buffers), and process them via programs called shaders. We need two different shaders to draw our triangle. The first is a vertex shader, which reads vertices from the VBO and transforms them if necessary. Second, is a fragment shader which calculates the colour for each pixel in the triangle.

If you have the Modern Graphics Programming Primer, then I highly recommend reading the following sections first:

- Overview of the Modern GPU

- Shaders

- Vertex Buffers

This will give you a good understanding of how the GPU works, and what it is you're doing. If you don't have the primer, then you can get it at: https://keasigmadelta.com/graphics-primer

Getting Started

Create a new project called GLTutorial2 following the procedure learned in "Tutorial 1: Getting Started." Next, copy and paste Tutorial 1's code into Main.cpp. We'll be using this as a starting point.

The Shaders

The Vertex Shader

Create a new source file called "Simple2D.vert" (NOTE: in Visual C++, use the C++ source file template, but make sure the file ends in ".vert"). Enter the following code:

```
#version 300 es

in vec2 vertPos;

out vec4 colour;

const vec4 white = vec4(1.0);

void main() {
    colour = white;
    gl_Position = vec4(vertPos, 0.0, 1.0);
}
```

Let's go through this one section at a time. The "*#version 300 es*" statement at the top indicates that this shader is written in GLSL version 3.0.0 for OpenGL ES.

The next two lines declare input and output variables:

```
in vec2 vertPos;

out vec4 colour;
```

So, the vertex shader takes a 2D vertex position as input, and outputs a 4 channel colour parameter. The colour output isn't really needed right now, but it demonstrates passing parameters from the vertex shader through to the fragment shader.

The next line creates a constant for the colour white:

```
const vec4 white = vec4(1.0);
```

The main() function is called for every vertex. The code simply sets the output colour to white, and copies the 2D position into *gl_Position* (which is a predefined output in GLSL):

```
void main() {
    colour = white;
    gl_Position = vec4(vertPos, 0.0, 1.0);
}
```

Vec4(vertPos, 0.0, 1.0) is the equivalent of *vec4(vertPos.x, vertPos.y, 0.0, 1.0)*. This is necessary because our input vector is 2D, whereas gl_Position is a 4D vector.

The Fragment Shader

Now create a file called "Simple2D.frag," and enter the following:

```
#version 300 es

#ifdef GL_ES
precision highp float;
#endif

in vec4 colour;

out vec4 fragColour;

void main() {
    fragColour = colour;
}
```

This simply takes the colour received from the vertex shader (via the rasterizer), and writes it to the output pixel (*fragColor*).

Compiling and Linking the Shaders

The shaders need to be compiled to the GPU's machine code, and then linked to form a shader program. An OpenGL shader program contains all shaders needed to go from vertices to rendered pixels (so both the vertex and fragment shader).

Let's put the shader handling code into its own separate source file. Organising a program into logical blocks is key to building large complicated systems, and we might as well start now. Plus, we'll be needing this code again and again so creating a separate module will make reusing it easier (just copy the files to the next project).

So, create two new source files: "Shader.cpp" and "Shader.h." For each file, right-click on "GLTutorial2" in the Solution Explorer (left column), and select Add => New Item...

NOTE: While the file suffix may be ".cpp," we will be using plain C (with C++'s stricter syntax requirements). I don't want to waste time explaining C++ classes because it would distract from your real goal, which is learning OpenGL.

The header file (Shader.h) provides an interface for other parts of the program to use. It declares two functions: shaderProgLoad() and shaderProgDestroy(). Other source files can use them by including this header, and calling those functions. Here's Shader.h's full listing:

```cpp
// Shader.h

#ifndef __SHADER_H__
#define __SHADER_H__

#include <GLES3/gl3.h>

/** Loads a vertex and fragment shader from disk and compiles (& links) them
 * into a shader program.
 *
 * This will print any errors to the console.
 *
 * @param vertFilename filename for the vertex shader
 * @param fragFilename the fragment shader's filename.
 *
 * @return GLuint the shader program's ID, or 0 if failed.
 */
GLuint shaderProgLoad(const char *vertFilename, const char *fragFilename);

/** Destroys a shader program.
 */
void shaderProgDestroy(GLuint shaderProg);

#endif
```

The actual code for these functions (a.k.a., the function definitions) are in Shader.cpp, along with any support code they need. Let's go through this file step-by-step.

First, we include Shader.h and other headers. Including Shader.h ensures that the function declarations and definitions match. The compiler will warn us if the two files ever get out of sync. Here's the code:

```
// Shader.cpp
//
// See header file for details

#include "Shader.h"

#include <cstdio>
#include <cstdlib>
#include <SDL.h>
#include <SDL_opengles2.h>

#ifdef _MSC_VER
#pragma warning(disable:4996) // Allows us to use the portable fopen()
                              // function without warnings
#endif
```

The line starting with #pragma is to disable warnings when using standard C file handling functions. Visual Studio warns that they're "unsafe," and provides Microsoft Windows specific alternatives. However, we want to stick to standard C so that the code can be used unchanged on other systems. So, the warning is disabled.

HINT: It's good practise to ensure that your code compiles with no warnings. That way you'll easily see genuine warnings instead of losing them in a sea of false ones.

Compiling a Single Shader

Next, we need a function to load a shader from disk. In turn, this function needs to be able to get the length of a file in bytes. So, we define another function called *fileGetLength()*:

```
/** Gets the file's length.
 *
 * @param file the file
 *
 * @return size_t the file's length in bytes
 */
static size_t fileGetLength(FILE *file) {
    size_t length;

    size_t currPos = ftell(file);
```

```
    fseek(file, 0, SEEK_END);
    length = ftell(file);

    // Return the file to its previous position
    fseek(file, currPos, SEEK_SET);

    return length;
}
```

This function scans through a file with *fseek()* and uses *ftell()* to get its size. These are standard C library functions. Look up the documentation for *fseek()* and *ftell()* to find out how they're used. You can find documentation for the entire standard C/C++ library here:

http://www.cplusplus.com/reference/

Now we can write the function to load and compile a shader (*shaderLoad()*):

```
/** Loads and compiles a shader from a file.
 *
 * This will print any errors to the console.
 *
 * @param filename the shader's filename
 * @param shaderType the shader type (e.g., GL_VERTEX_SHADER)
 *
 * @return GLuint the shader's ID, or 0 if failed
 */
static GLuint shaderLoad(const char *filename, GLenum shaderType) {
    FILE *file = fopen(filename, "r");
    if (!file) {
        SDL_Log("Can't open file: %s\n", filename);

        return 0;
    }

    size_t length = fileGetLength(file);

    // Alloc space for the file (plus '\0' termination)
    GLchar *shaderSrc = (GLchar*)calloc(length + 1, 1);
    if (!shaderSrc) {
        SDL_Log("Out of memory when reading file: %s\n", filename);
```

```c
    fclose(file);
    file = NULL;

    return 0;
}

fread(shaderSrc, 1, length, file);

// Done with the file
fclose(file);
file = NULL;

// Create the shader
GLuint shader = glCreateShader(shaderType);
glShaderSource(shader, 1, (const GLchar**)&shaderSrc, NULL);
free(shaderSrc);
shaderSrc = NULL;

// Compile it
glCompileShader(shader);
GLint compileSucceeded = GL_FALSE;
glGetShaderiv(shader, GL_COMPILE_STATUS, &compileSucceeded);
if (!compileSucceeded) {
    // Compilation failed. Print error info
    SDL_Log("Compilation of shader %s failed:\n", filename);
    GLint logLength = 0;
    glGetShaderiv(shader, GL_INFO_LOG_LENGTH, &logLength);
    GLchar *errLog = (GLchar*)malloc(logLength);
    if (errLog) {
        glGetShaderInfoLog(shader, logLength, &logLength, errLog);
        SDL_Log("%s\n", errLog);
        free(errLog);
    }
    else {
        SDL_Log("Couldn't get shader log; out of memory\n");
    }

    glDeleteShader(shader);
    shader = 0;
}
```

```
    return shader;
}
```

This is a fairly long function, so here's an overview. The first section (up to *fclose()*) loads the shader file into a buffer. Next, an empty shader is created (*glCreateShader()*), the source-code is added (*glShaderSource()*), and is compiled (*glCompileShader()*). After that, we check whether compilation succeeded (*glGetShaderiv()* with *GL_COMPILE_STATUS*), and get the compilation log if it failed (*glGetShaderInfoLog()*). SDL provides a convenient platform-independent method to print the log called *SDL_Log()*.

Accompanying *shaderLoad()* is *shaderDestroy()*, which deletes a shader once it's no longer needed:

```
/** Destroys a shader.
 */
static void shaderDestroy(GLuint shaderID) {
    glDeleteShader(shaderID);
}
```

It might seem redundant to create a function that simply calls another function, but the code is clearer this way. *ShaderLoad()* and *shaderDestroy()* form a logical pair; no need to go searching for the correct function to destroy/delete a shader that's no longer needed.

Linking Shaders into a Program

Okay, we can load individual shaders. Now they need to be linked into a shader program. Shader.h declared a function called shaderProgLoad() which loads a vertex and fragment shader, and then links them together. Time to write the actual code:

```
GLuint shaderProgLoad(const char *vertFilename, const char *fragFilename) {
    GLuint vertShader = shaderLoad(vertFilename, GL_VERTEX_SHADER);
    if (!vertShader) {
        SDL_Log("Couldn't load vertex shader: %s\n", vertFilename);

        return 0;
    }

    GLuint fragShader = shaderLoad(fragFilename, GL_FRAGMENT_SHADER);
    if (!fragShader) {
        SDL_Log("Couldn't load fragment shader: %s\n", fragFilename);
```

```c
        shaderDestroy(vertShader);
        vertShader = 0;

        return 0;
    }


    GLuint shaderProg = glCreateProgram();
    if (shaderProg) {
        glAttachShader(shaderProg, vertShader);
        glAttachShader(shaderProg, fragShader);

        glLinkProgram(shaderProg);

        GLint linkingSucceeded = GL_FALSE;
        glGetProgramiv(shaderProg, GL_LINK_STATUS, &linkingSucceeded);
        if (!linkingSucceeded) {
            SDL_Log("Linking shader failed "
                "(vert. shader: %s, frag. shader: %s\n",
                vertFilename, fragFilename);
            GLint logLength = 0;
            glGetProgramiv(shaderProg, GL_INFO_LOG_LENGTH, &logLength);
            GLchar *errLog = (GLchar*)malloc(logLength);
            if (errLog) {
                glGetProgramInfoLog(shaderProg, logLength, &logLength,
                    errLog);
                SDL_Log("%s\n", errLog);
                free(errLog);
            }
            else {
                SDL_Log("Couldn't get shader link log; out of memory\n");
            }
            glDeleteProgram(shaderProg);
            shaderProg = 0;
        }
    }
    else {
        SDL_Log("Couldn't create shader program\n");
    }

    // Don't need these any more
```

```
    shaderDestroy(vertShader);
    shaderDestroy(fragShader);

    return shaderProg;
}
```

This function starts by loading the two shaders (*shaderLoad()*). If that's successful then it creates a shader program (*glCreateProgram()*), attaches the shaders to the program (*glAttachShader()*), and links them (*glLinkProgram()*). Next, it checks if linking succeeded (*glGetProgramiv()* with *GL_LINK_STATUS*) and prints out an error log obtained via *glGetProgramInfoLog()*. If linking succeeded, then the shader objects can be deleted (*shaderDestroy()*). Finally, the newly created shader program is returned to the code that called *shaderProgLoad()*.

As with *shaderLoad()*, *shaderProgLoad()* has a matching *shaderProgDestroy()*:

```
void shaderProgDestroy(GLuint shaderProg) {
    glDeleteProgram(shaderProg);
}
```

With *shaderProgDestroy()* created, Shader.cpp is complete.

Activating the Shader

Okay, that's the low-level mechanics of compiling and linking shaders taken care of. Now, let's put it to use. Switch back to "Main.cpp," and add the following include to the top (where the other includes are):

```
#include "Shader.h"
```

This allows us to call the functions declared in "Shader.h" from "Main.cpp." Next, scroll down to the main() function, and insert the following code below the SDL_GL_SwapWindow() call:

```
    // Load the shader program and set it for use
    GLuint shaderProg = shaderProgLoad("Simple2D.vert", "Simple2D.frag");
    if (!shaderProg) {
        // Error messages already displayed...
        return EXIT_FAILURE;
    }
    glUseProgram(shaderProg);
```

The first line calls *shaderProgLoad()* to load the shader program, while the *glUseProgram()* call activates the shader. Any draw calls made from now on will use our shaders.

Creating the Triangle

The code above sets up shaders so that we can draw stuff, but we still need something to draw. For this tutorial we're going to draw a simple triangle. Most tutorial series would teach you the easiest way to do this first, and later tell you "don't do it that way, use this method instead." So you end up learning how to draw a triangle multiple times.

I'm going to teach you the preferred way immediately. Yes, it takes more effort, but this is the method you should be using in production code. We're going to store the triangle's vertices in a Vertex Buffer Object (VBO). Why? Because that allows us to store it in video RAM, where the GPU has fastest access (and can therefore deliver highest performance).

Here's a function to create a VBO for some vertices:

```
/** Creates the Vertex Buffer Object (VBO) containing
 * the given vertices.
 *
 * @param vertices pointer to the array of vertices
 * @param numVertices the number of vertices in the array
 */
GLuint vboCreate(const Vertex *vertices, GLuint numVertices) {
    // Create the Vertex Buffer Object
    GLuint vbo;
    int nBuffers = 1;
    glGenBuffers(nBuffers, &vbo);
    glBindBuffer(GL_ARRAY_BUFFER, vbo);

    // Copy the vertex data in, and deactivate
    glBufferData(GL_ARRAY_BUFFER, sizeof(Vertex) * numVertices, vertices,
        GL_STATIC_DRAW);
    glBindBuffer(GL_ARRAY_BUFFER, 0);

    // Check for problems
    GLenum err = glGetError();
    if (err != GL_NO_ERROR) {
        // Failed
        glDeleteBuffers(nBuffers, &vbo);
```

```
        SDL_Log("Creating VBO failed, code %u\n", err);
        vbo = 0;
    }

    return vbo;
}
```

This function will take an array of *vertices* that's *numVertices* long, and create a VBO to store them. *GlGenBuffers()* creates the buffer, *glBindBuffer()* with *GL_ARRAY_BUFFER* makes it a VBO, and *glBufferData()* copies the data in. *GlBufferData()*'s last parameter is *GL_STATIC_DRAW*. This is a hint to OpenGL that the buffer should be stored in VRAM because its contents will be used over and over without being changed.

As with previous code, *vboCreate()* should have a matching destroy function:

```
/** Frees the VBO.
 *
 * @param vbo the VBO's name.
 */
void vboFree(GLuint vbo) {
    glDeleteBuffers(1, &vbo);
}
```

The Actual Triangle

Time to put *vboCreate()* to use, and create the actual triangle. First, we need to define what a vertex is. This must match the input to the vertex shader. So, insert the following just below the #include lines in Main.cpp:

```
/** Encapsulates the data for a single vertex.
 * Must match the vertex shader's input.
 */
typedef struct Vertex_s {
    float position[2];
} Vertex;
```

The code above defines a *Vertex* that has a 2D position. Next, insert the following code in *main()*, below the *glUseProgram()* call (in Main.cpp):

```
    // Create the triangle
```

```
const Vertex vertices[] = {
    { 0.0f, -0.9f },
    { 0.9f,  0.9f },
    {-0.9f,  0.9f } };
GLsizei vertSize = sizeof(vertices[0]);
GLsizei numVertices = sizeof(vertices) / vertSize;
GLuint triangleVBO = vboCreate(vertices, numVertices);
if (!triangleVBO) {
    // Failed. Error message has already been printed, so just quit
    return EXIT_FAILURE;
}
```

The *vertices* array contains the actual vertex data, and the code below creates the VBO.

Drawing the Triangle

Drawing is a two-step process. First the OpenGL state needs to be set up. We started this before by activating our shader with *glUseProgram()* (already done above). Next, we tell OpenGL where to find the vertex data, as follows:

```
// Set up for rendering the triangle (activate the VBO)
GLuint positionIdx = 0; // Position is vertex attribute 0
glBindBuffer(GL_ARRAY_BUFFER, triangleVBO);
glVertexAttribPointer(positionIdx, 2, GL_FLOAT, GL_FALSE,
    sizeof(Vertex), (const GLvoid*)0);
glEnableVertexAttribArray(positionIdx);
```

Let's go through this line by line. OpenGL can read multiple vertex attributes (e.g., position, texture coordinates, etc.). *PositionIdx* is the index of the position attribute. We know that *positionIdx* is 0 because the vertex shader (*Simple2D.vert*) has only one vertex input.

Next, *glBindBuffer()* is called, which tells OpenGL that subsequent calls to *glVertexAttribPointer()* should use *triangleVBO*. Thus, the *glVertexAttribPointer()* call sets up the position (*positionIdx*) to be read from *triangleVBO* starting at offset *0* (the last parameter: *(const GLvoid*)0*), with a stride between vertices of *sizeof(Vertex)* bytes.

Finally, the position attribute is enabled with *glEnableVertexAttribArray()*.

Now that OpenGL knows where to read the triangle from, we can finally render it with one line of code:

```
// Now draw!
glDrawArrays(GL_TRIANGLES, 0, numVertices);
```

Don't forget to flip the buffers as well, to display the final image:

```
// Update the window
SDL_GL_SwapWindow(window);
```

That's it! The triangle is drawn.

Cleanup

Modern software is good at cleaning up all resources on exit, but it's still good to get into the habit of doing this manually. If anything, your software should free/deallocate resources that it no longer needs (e.g., 3D models for a game level that just finished).

Insert the following cleanup code just before *main()*'s final return statement. It frees the VBO and disposes of the shader program:

```
// Cleanup
vboFree(triangleVBO);
triangleVBO = 0;
shaderProgDestroy(shaderProg);
shaderProg = 0;
```

Testing

Save everything, then compile and run it. If you did everything correctly, then you should be greeted with a white triangle (Figure 7). Congratulations on your first OpenGL render!

If you didn't see a white triangle, then go back and compare your code carefully with the code in the tutorial above.

HINT: If the program exits immediately, then check the error messages printed to the console by *SDL_Log()*. In Visual Studio (and other IDEs) those log messages typically go to an "Output" sub-window at the bottom of the screen.

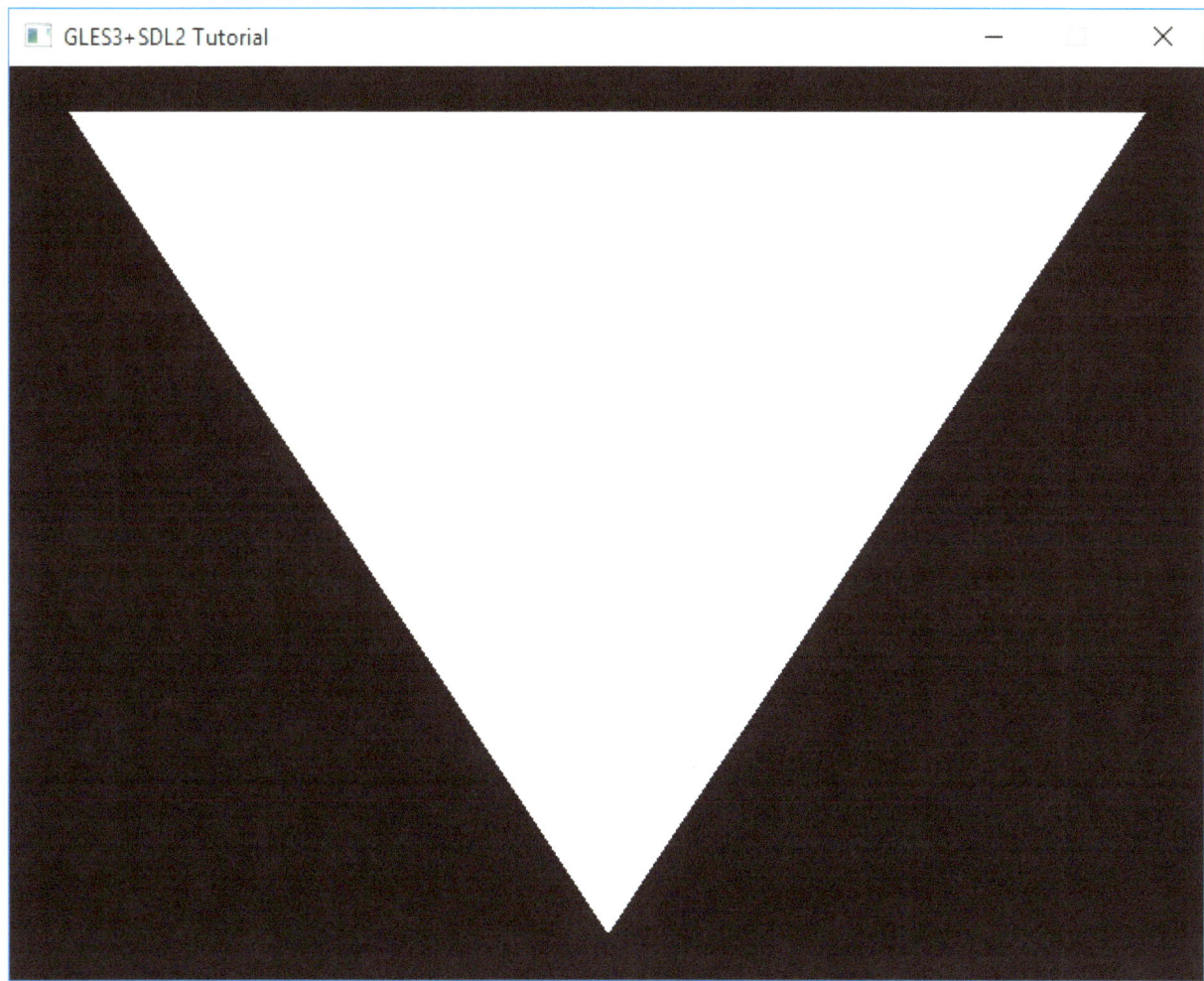

Figure 7: Our first render; a white triangle.

Exercises

Time to experiment and write your own code. See if you can do the following:

1. Go through the code step by step, and make sure you understand what it's doing. Look up the documentation for any function you're not sure about. Here are some useful links:

   ○ C/C++ Standard Library Reference: http://www.cplusplus.com/reference/

- ○ OpenGL ES 3 Reference:
  https://www.khronos.org/opengles/sdk/docs/man3/html/index.php

2. Change the triangle's colour to red, blue, green, yellow, or some other colour

3. Change the triangle's size and shape

   HINT: Modify the *vertices* array in *main()*

4. Draw a second triangle

5. Draw a second triangle using one VBO and one draw call

   HINT: Multiple triangles fit in a VBO, and *glDrawArrays()* can render many triangles in one go

6. Change the vertex shader so that the colour is related to the position. The triangle should have a colour gradient

   HINT: Colour values are in the range [0,1], so you may need to perform arithmetic operations to scale and shift the position before writing it to the *colour* variable

Tutorial 3: Texture Mapping

Most OpenGL tutorial series would now have a tutorial that adds per-vertex colours. However, that's rather boring, and per-vertex colouring isn't all that useful. So let's jump straight to texture mapping instead. This will mean more work, but the results will be worth it.

Texture mapping is basically wrapping a 3D model with an image. This is an easy way to add more detail (a.k.a., texture) to an object. We'll be using it to draw a wooden box.

HINT: For more, look at the "Texture Mapping" section in the "Modern Graphics Programming Primer" (https://keasigmadelta.com/graphics-primer)

Getting Started

Start by creating a new project called GLTutorial3. Use the same method you've used for previous tutorials. Now copy GLTutorial2's source files: Main.cpp and Shader.cpp|h, and add them to the project (right-click on GLTutorial3, and select Add => Existing item...). We'll be building on those.

Neither SDL2 nor OpenGL come with functions to load images, so we're going to use a new library called SDL_image.

Installing SDL_image on Windows

Select Tools => NuGet Package Manager => Package Manager Console from the menus (Figure 8).

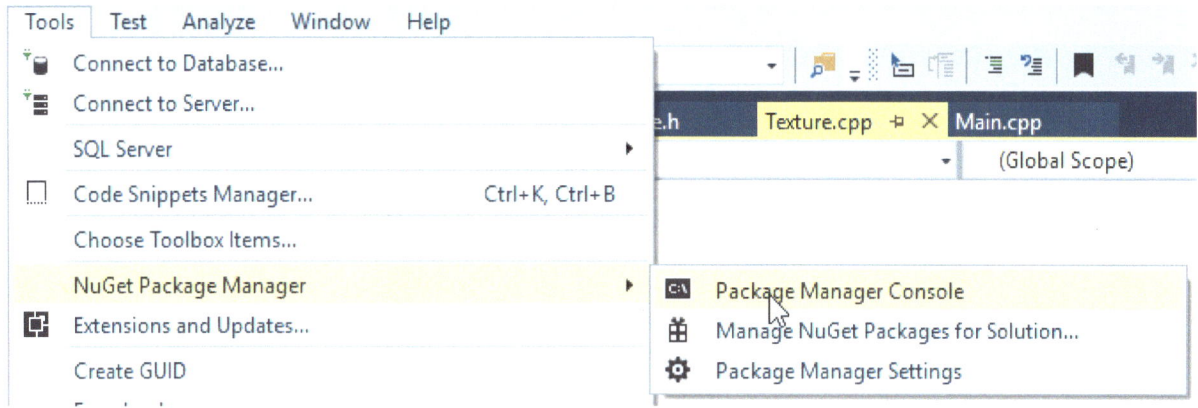

Figure 8: Opening the NuGet Package Manager Console.

The console will open at the bottom of the window. Now type the following, and push enter (Figure 9):

```
Install-Package sdl2_image.v140
```

SDL_image is now installed into the project and ready to go.

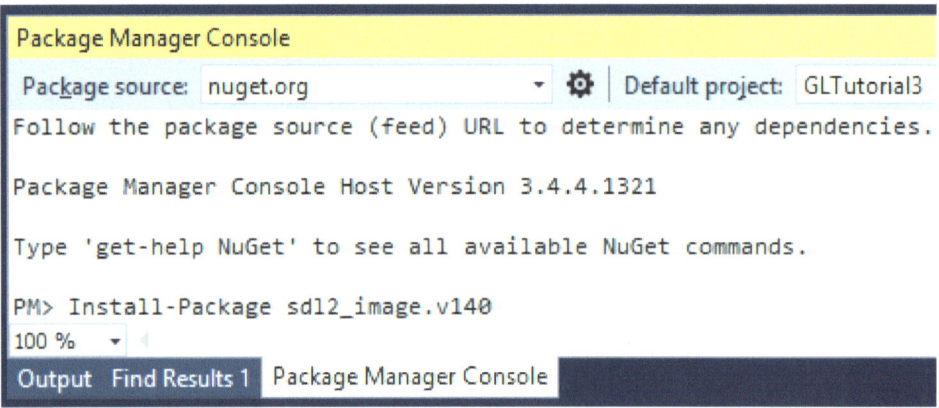

Figure 9: Installing SDL_image via NuGet.

Installing SDL_image on Other Platforms

If you're using another OS, then you'll need to look up how to install SDL_image.

Texture Mapping Shaders

New shaders are needed for texture mapping. For starters, each vertex needs a texture coordinate, which indicates what part of the texture appears at that point. Next, the fragment shader has to actually read the texture. Here's how it's done...

The Vertex Shader

Create a new file called Texture.vert, and enter the following code:

```
#version 300 es

layout(location = 0) in vec2 vertPos;
layout(location = 1) in vec2 vertTexCoord;
```

```
out vec2 texCoord;

void main() {
    texCoord = vertTexCoord;
    gl_Position = vec4(vertPos, 0.0, 1.0);
}
```

The code is still very basic; it just passes the vertex coordinates straight through. There are a few things to pay attention to, though.

First, there are now two inputs (a.k.a., vertex attributes): the vertex position (*vertexPos*), and the texture coordinates (*vertTexCoord)*. This means we now have two vertex attribute arrays to set up. We'll do that in the Vertex Texture Coordinates section below (Page 45).

Second, the inputs have been given explicit locations using *layout(location = n)*. This very handy feature was introduced in OpenGL ES 3, and allows us to specify which vertex attribute each input is mapped to. Before, we'd have to get or set the vertex attribute to shader variable mappings manually in the main code. This was rather tedious, so being able to set them in the shader code is awesome.

The Fragment Shader

Here's the code to enter into *Texture.frag*:

```
#version 300 es

#ifdef GL_ES
precision highp float;
#endif

in vec2 texCoord;

out vec4 fragColour;

uniform sampler2D texSampler;

void main() {
    fragColour = texture(texSampler, texCoord);
}
```

This is the simplest shader capable of reading textures. It has the three essentials: a texture sampler (*texSampler*), the texture coordinate to read (*texCoord*) and a *texture()* function call. The texture's colour at *texCoord* is written straight to the output: *fragColour*.

Binding the Sampler2D to a Texture Unit

I had really hoped to skip this step via an OpenGL ES 3.1 feature that allows you to set the texture unit in the GLSL shader code. Alas, the Angle library doesn't support this yet, so we're stuck doing it the version 3.0 way. I'll update this tutorial once this issue has been fixed.

In *Main.cpp*, add the following code below the *shaderLoad()* section:

```
// Bind texSampler to unit 0
GLint texSamplerUniformLoc = glGetUniformLocation(shaderProg,
    "texSampler");
if (texSamplerUniformLoc < 0) {
    SDL_Log("ERROR: Couldn't get texSampler's location.");
    return EXIT_FAILURE;
}
glUniform1i(texSamplerUniformLoc, 0);
```

This code gets the vertex shader's *texSampler* variable, and sets it to *0* for texture unit *0*.

While you're working on this code, you may as well update the *shaderLoad()* call to load our new shaders:

```
GLuint shaderProg = shaderProgLoad("Texture.vert", "Texture.frag");
```

Texture Loading

Okay, the shaders are ready. Now we have to load the actual texture into video memory. Actually, first we need a texture. There are plenty of textures available online (both free and not). You can use whatever you wish. I'll be using a wooden crate texture that's available here: http://opengameart.org/content/3-crate-textures-w-bump-normal

Once you've downloaded and unzipped the file, copy crate1/crate1_diffuse.png to GLTutorial3/GLTutorial3/. Don't worry about the other files; we won't be using them.

Now, on to loading the texture. Create two files, *Texture.cpp* and its header called *Texture.h*. We're going to write a function to load textures (*texLoad()*), and one to free the texture at the end (*texDestroy()*). Here's the resulting header file (Texture.h):

```cpp
// Texture.h

#ifndef __TEXTURE_H__
#define __TEXTURE_H__

#include <GLES3/gl3.h>

/** Loads a 2D texture from file.
 *
 * @param filename name of the image file to load
 *
 * @return GLuint the texture's name, or 0 if failed
 */
GLuint texLoad(const char *filename);

/** Deallocates a texture.
 */
void texDestroy(GLuint texName);

#endif
```

Now switch to Texture.cpp. Start by including the header files we'll need:

```cpp
// Texture.cpp
//
// See header file for details

#include "Texture.h"

#include <SDL.h>
#include <SDL_image.h>
#include <SDL_opengles2.h>
```

Swizzling

The texture loader will need one support function, called *sdlToGLSwizzle()*. This will transform SDL colour channel masks to OpenGL "swizzles." Swizzling maps image channels to texture inputs. For example, an image may have the colours stored in ARGB order, which need to be mapped to the texture unit's RGBA channels. Here's how it's done:

```
/** Sets the swizzling for a texture colour channel from an SDL colour mask.
 *
 * @param channel the texture channel to set (e.g., GL_TEXTURE_SWIZZLE_R)
 * @param mask the SDL colour channel mask (e.g., texSurf->format->Rmask)
 */

bool sdlToGLSwizzle(GLenum channel, Uint32 mask) {
    GLint swizzle;
    switch (mask) {
    case 0x000000FF:
#if SDL_BYTEORDER == SDL_BIG_ENDIAN
            swizzle = GL_ALPHA;
#else
            swizzle = GL_RED;
#endif
        break;
    case 0x0000FF00:
#if SDL_BYTEORDER == SDL_BIG_ENDIAN
            swizzle = GL_BLUE;
#else
            swizzle = GL_GREEN;
#endif
        break;
    case 0x00FF0000:
#if SDL_BYTEORDER == SDL_BIG_ENDIAN
            swizzle = GL_GREEN;
#else
            swizzle = GL_BLUE;
#endif
        break;
    case 0xFF000000:
#if SDL_BYTEORDER == SDL_BIG_ENDIAN
            swizzle = GL_ALPHA;
```

```
#else
            swizzle = GL_RED;
#endif
        break;
    default:
        SDL_Log("Unrecognized colour channel mask 0x%08X", mask);
        return false;
    }

    glTexParameteri(GL_TEXTURE_2D, channel, swizzle);
    return true;
}
```

The code is designed to support both big and little-endian processors. If you don't know what that means, don't worry about it for now (or look it up online). What's important is that *glTexParameteri()* is given the correct channel to read from.

Confusingly, OpenGL uses *GL_RED*, *GL_GREEN*, *GL_BLUE*, & *GL_ALPHA* instead of channel numbers. So you can end up with the "red" channel being read from *GL_ALPHA*, etc. I've been caught out by this, so my advice is to make sure you keep backups once you have code that works.

Loading the Texture

Let's move on to the actual texture loading. SDL_image is used to load the image, and then *glTexImage2D()* is used to turn it into an OpenGL texture:

```
GLuint texLoad(const char *filename) {
    // Make sure the JPEG and PNG image loaders are present (don't know what
    // file type we'll get).
    int flags = IMG_INIT_JPG | IMG_INIT_PNG;
    if ((IMG_Init(flags) & flags) == 0) {
        // Failed :-(
        SDL_Log("ERROR: Texture loading failed. "
            "Couldn't get JPEG & PNG loaders.\n");
        return 0;
    }

    // Load the image
    SDL_Surface *texSurf = IMG_Load(filename);
    if (!texSurf) {
```

```cpp
        SDL_Log("Loading image %s failed with error: %s",
            filename, IMG_GetError());
        return 0;
    }

    // Determine the format
    // NOTE: Only supporting 24 and 32-bit images
    GLenum format;
    GLenum type = GL_UNSIGNED_BYTE;
    switch (texSurf->format->BytesPerPixel) {
    case 3:
        format = GL_RGB;
        break;
    case 4:
        format = GL_RGBA;
        break;
    default:
        SDL_Log(
            "Can't load image %s; it isn't a 24/32-bit image\n", filename);
        SDL_FreeSurface(texSurf);
        texSurf = NULL;
        return 0;
    }

    // Create the texture
    GLuint texture;
    glGenTextures(1, &texture);
    glBindTexture(GL_TEXTURE_2D, texture);
    glTexImage2D(GL_TEXTURE_2D, 0, format, texSurf->w,
        texSurf->h, 0, format, type, texSurf->pixels);
    GLenum err = glGetError();
    if (err != GL_NO_ERROR) {
        // Failed
        glDeleteBuffers(1, &texture);
        texture = 0;
        SDL_FreeSurface(texSurf);
        texSurf = NULL;
        SDL_Log("Creating texture %s failed, code %u\n", filename, err);
        return 0;
    }
```

```cpp
    // Set up texture swizzling to match the image's channel order
    bool success = sdlToGLSwizzle(GL_TEXTURE_SWIZZLE_R,
        texSurf->format->Rmask);
    success &= sdlToGLSwizzle(GL_TEXTURE_SWIZZLE_G, texSurf->format->Gmask);
    success &= sdlToGLSwizzle(GL_TEXTURE_SWIZZLE_B, texSurf->format->Bmask);
    if (format == GL_RGBA) {
        success &= sdlToGLSwizzle(GL_TEXTURE_SWIZZLE_A,
            texSurf->format->Amask);
    }
    if (!success) {
        SDL_Log("Couldn't set up swizzling for texture %s\n", filename);
        glDeleteBuffers(1, &texture);
        texture = 0;
        SDL_FreeSurface(texSurf);
        texSurf = NULL;
        return 0;
    }

    // Set up the filtering
    // NOTE: Failure to do this may result in no texture
    glTexParameteri(GL_TEXTURE_2D, GL_TEXTURE_MAG_FILTER, GL_LINEAR);
    glTexParameteri(GL_TEXTURE_2D, GL_TEXTURE_MIN_FILTER, GL_LINEAR);

    // Cleanup
    SDL_FreeSurface(texSurf);
    texSurf = NULL;

    return texture;
}
```

This is a long function, so let's take a look at the key steps. First, SDL_image is initialised (*IMG_Init()*). Next, the image is loaded (*IMG_load()*). If that's successful then a texture object is created (*glGenTextures()*), made active (*glBindTexture()*) and the image data is uploaded into the texture (*glTexImage2D()*). The call to glBindTexture() is necessary because *glTexImage2D()* uploads to the current texture object; it has no parameter to specify which texture to upload to.

Once the texture data is uploaded, the swizzling is set for all colour channels by calling our *sdlToGLSwizzle()* function. Next, the texture "filtering" is set up (*glTexParameteri()* with *GL_TEXTURE_MAG_FILTER* and *GL_TEXTURE_MIN_FILTER*). You may end up with no image if you skip this, even though those settings should be *GL_LINEAR* by default.[1]

Finally, the original image data is no longer needed, so it's freed with *SDL_FreeSurface()*.

Destroying/Deleting The Texture

Deleting the texture is really easy, making *texDestroy()* nice and short:

```
void texDestroy(GLuint texName) {
    glDeleteTextures(1, &texName);
}
```

Using the Texture

Nearly there! Switch back to Main.cpp. At the top, add a line to include Texture.h so that we can use *texLoad()*/*texDestroy()*:

```
#include "Texture.h"
```

Now scroll down to main(), and insert the following code to load the box texture. Be sure to insert it somewhere after *SDL_GL_CreateContext()* (I recommend putting it after the code to load the shaders).

```
    // Load the texture
    GLuint texture = texLoad("crate1_diffuse.png");
    if (!texture) {
        SDL_ShowSimpleMessageBox(SDL_MESSAGEBOX_ERROR, "Error",
            "Couldn't load texture.", NULL);
        return EXIT_FAILURE;
    }

    // Bind the texture to unit 0
    glActiveTexture(GL_TEXTURE0);
    glBindTexture(GL_TEXTURE_2D, texture);
```

---

1   Have a look at the "Texture Filtering/Smoothing" section of the "Modern Graphics Programming Primer" for an explanation of texture filtering: https://keasigmadelta.com/graphics-primer

This code loads the texture (*texLoad()*), and then bind it to texture unit 0 (via *glActiveTexture()* and *glBindTexture()*).

NOTE: The *glActiveTexture()* call is actually redundant, because it's 0 by default. I'm including because forgetting to set/reset the texture unit can cause confusing bugs.

Finally, scroll down to the "Cleanup" section at the end, and add code to delete the texture:

```
texDestroy(texture);
texture = 0;
```

Vertex Texture Coordinates

Okay, we now have code to load and use textures (including texture-mapping shader code), but we're not quite done yet. The vertices need a texture-coordinate to indicate what part of the texture goes where.

In *Main.cpp*, scroll back up to find the *Vertex* typedef, and update it to:

```
/** Encapsulates the data for a single vertex.
 * Must match the vertex shader's input.
 */
typedef struct Vertex_s {
    float position[2];
    float texCoord[2];
} Vertex;
```

As you can see, the vertex now has two attributes; a position and a texture coordinate (*texCoord*). Next, update the vertices array in *main()*. Boxes are rectangular, so there are now four vertices instead of three:

```
// Create the quad/tri-fan
const Vertex vertices[] = {
    {{-0.9f, -0.9f}, {0.0f, 0.0f}},
    {{ 0.9f, -0.9f}, {1.0f, 0.0f}},
    {{ 0.9f,  0.9f}, {1.0f, 1.0f}},
    {{-0.9f,  0.9f}, {0.0f, 1.0f}}};
```

Almost done! We just need to tell OpenGL where to find the *texCoord* data. Find the line that sets the position pointer (with *glVertexAttribPointer()*), and add the following:

```
GLuint texCoordIdx = 1;  // TexCoord is vertex attribute 1
glVertexAttribPointer(texCoordIdx, 2, GL_FLOAT, GL_FALSE,
    sizeof(Vertex), (const GLvoid*)offsetof(Vertex, texCoord));
glEnableVertexAttribArray(texCoordIdx);
```

The key difference with the texture coordinate, is that *glVertexAttribPointer()*'s final parameter is *offsetof(Vertex, texCoord)* instead of *0*. This is critical, as it tells OpenGL to read the texture coord starting *offsetof(Vertex, texCoord)* bytes from the start of the VBO. The *offsetof()* function/macro is an easy way to calculate that offset. It'll also automatically recalculate the offset if we insert new fields into *Vertex*.

Draw

One more step, and then we're done! We're rendering a "quad" or triangle-fan instead of individual triangles. So change the glDrawArrays() call to do just that:

```
glDrawArrays(GL_TRIANGLE_FAN, 0, numVertices);
```

Now save everything, then compile and run the program. All going well, you should see the wooden box (Figure 10).

Figure 10: A texture-mapped wooden box.

Exercises

Time to experiment and write some code on your own. See if you can do the following:

1. Change the texture to something else

2. Change the box's dimensions (e.g., make it more square)

3. Change the fragment shader to flip the texture's y-axis coordinate (or t-axis; texture coordinates are usually denoted as (s, t) instead of (x, y))

   HINT: Perform a calculation on *texCoord* and pass the result to the *texture()* function

4. Render two identical boxes side-by-side

   HINT: Enable texture wrapping using *glTexParameteri()* with GL_TEXTURE_WRAP_T, and adjust the texture coordinates to suit

5. Render two different boxes with different textures

   HINT: You'll need to create two textures and add a new set of vertex coordinates. It is possible to add the vertices to the same VBO if you're smart about what you pass to *glDrawArrays()*

Tutorial 4: 3D At Last

Everything we've done so far has been in two dimensions (2D). I did this deliberately to keep things simple. Now it's time to make the jump to 3D (finally). It's a big jump though, so brace yourself...

The Theory

This tutorial isn't intended to be an in-depth course on 3D geometry & mathematics, so I'll keep this brief. Here, I'll only cover the bare minimum needed to get started. If you want more detail (recommended), then read the "3D Transformations and Coordinate Systems" section of the Modern Graphics Programming Primer (https://keasigmadelta.com/graphics-primer).

To render 3D objects onto a 2D screen we must build a world of 3D objects, and then simulate a camera that views it. We'd also very much like to animate objects, and allow everything to move freely. This is achieved via a set of different coordinate systems. Transformation matrices are used to convert from one set of coordinates to another.

First up, is the *model's coordinate system* (a.k.a., model space). A 3D model's vertices are stored as vectors relative to a common origin (often the object's centre). Why do this? Well, we can move the object around a 3D world by changing the m*odel matrix* (**M**), which transforms the points from model coordinates to world coordinates. We can also easily rotate the object about its own origin. Each model/object has its own local coordinates.

The world coordinate system is next. This is the global space that both 3D objects and the camera exist in. It's the global reference that everything else is relative to.

Next, the camera has its own coordinates, known as *view space*, and it views the world relative to the camera's origin. Objects & vertices are transformed from world to view space via the *view matrix* (**V**). This matrix is the inverse to what it would be for an object because it's transforming from world space rather than to it (which is what the model matrix does).

Finally, objects are projected from view space onto the 2D screen via a *projection matrix* (**P**). Actually, it's a bit more complicated than that (projection involves division), but you don't need to know the details to use it.

There's also a clip-space between the view space and screen. All you need to know about this is that it rejects everything that the camera can't see (e.g., what's behind and next to the camera).

The **M**, **V**, & **P** matrices can be multiplied together to form a single transformation from object to screen space:

$$\mathbf{p_s} = \mathbf{PVMp_0}$$

This is called the **MVP** matrix, although, as you can see above the matrices are multiplied in reverse order. It's a little confusing, so here's a good way to look at it. The vertex position $\mathbf{p_0}$ is on the far right, and it's transformed first by the matrix to its immediate left (**M**), then the next (**V**), and the next (**P**).

Getting Started

Create a new project using the same method as in previous tutorials, and call it GLTutorial4. Next, copy the GLTutorial3 code: Shader.cpp|h, Texture.cpp|h, texture.vert|frag, and Main.cpp, and add them to the project. Also copy the texture file over (crate1_diffuse.png).

SDL_image also needs to be installed into the project (if you're using Visual Studio and NuGet). So type the following into the NuGet Package Manager Console, and press enter:

```
Install-Package sdl2_image.v140
```

3D Mathematics

We need some kind of matrix/vector algebra library to perform the 3D transformations. While it is possible to write your own (done that myself), I recommend using a ready-made one. There are several well written open-source libraries available.

Here, we'll be using a C++ matrix library called GLM (openGL Mathematics).[2] It's designed specifically for OpenGL. Visual Studio users can install by entering the following in the NuGet Package Manager Console:

```
Install-Package GLMathematics
```

For some reason Visual Studio can't find the installed header files (at least on my system), so you may have to add the directory manually. Right-click on GLTutorial4, and select properties, select

---

2   GLM: http://glm.g-truc.net/0.9.8/index.html.

"VC++ Directories," and add the GLM include directory to the "Include Directories" (Figure 11). Here's the full include directories line I ended up with:

```
angle\include;..\packages\GLMathematics.0.9.5.4\build\native\incl
ude;$(IncludePath)
```

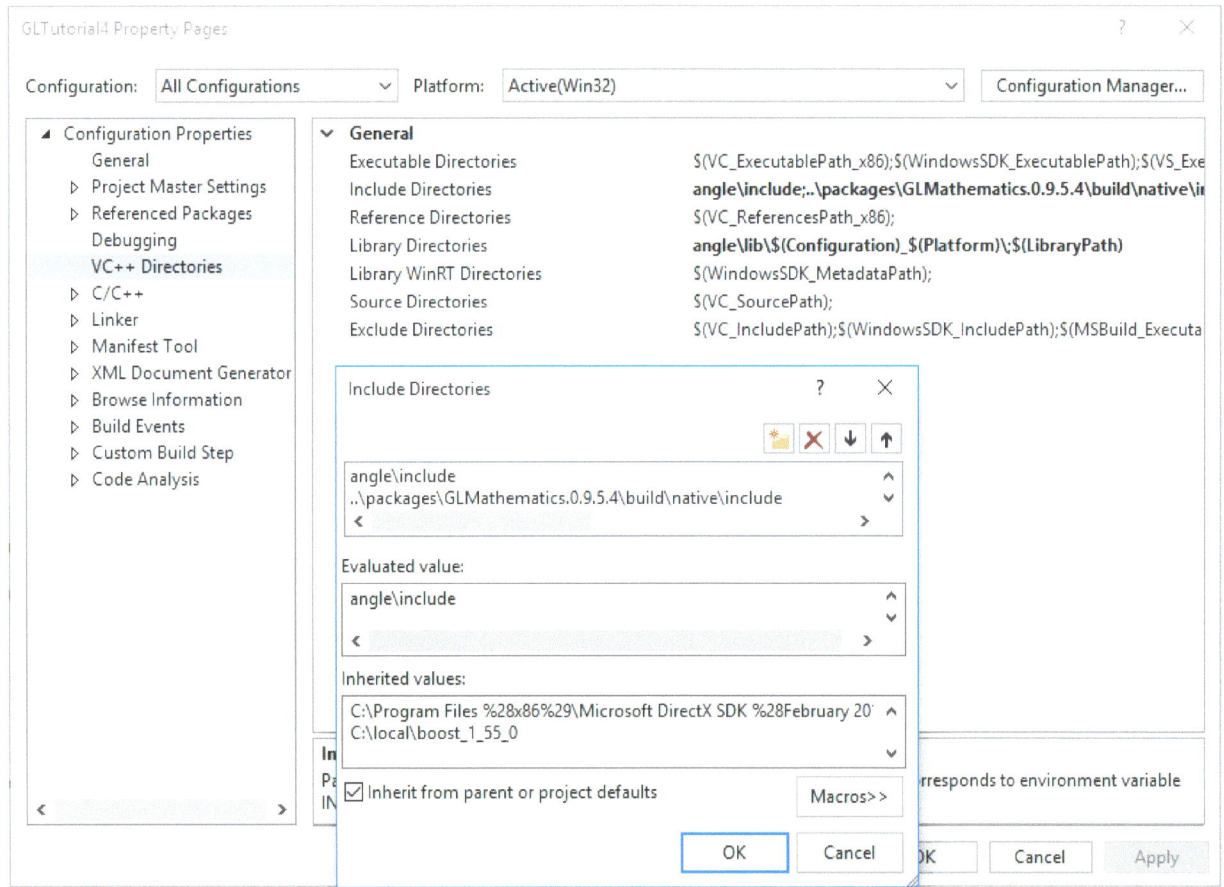

Figure 11: Adding the GLM includes manually.

Users of other platforms can download GLM from its project page: http://glm.g-truc.net/0.9.8/index.html

Installation is really easy because it's a header only project (i.e., there's nothing to compile). Simply copy the header files and add them to your project.

MVP Matrix in the Vertex Shader

As explained in the theory section above, the 3D model's vertices will be transformed from model space to view space, and then projected via the **MVP** matrix. Our existing texture.vert shader needs a few tweaks to be able to do this. First, the vertex position must be three dimensional, not 2D:

```
layout(location = 0) in vec3 vertPos;
```

Next, add an *MVPMatrix* uniform variable:

```
uniform mat4 MVPMatrix;
```

Finally, *vertexPos* must be (pre)multiplied by *MVPMatrix* to perform the transformation and projection:

```
    gl_Position = MVPMatrix * vec4(vertPos, 1.0);
```

Here's the resulting shader in full:

```
#version 300 es

layout(location = 0) in vec3 vertPos;
layout(location = 1) in vec2 vertTexCoord;

out vec2 texCoord;

uniform mat4 mvpMatrix;

void main() {
    texCoord = vertTexCoord;
    gl_Position = mvpMatrix * vec4(vertPos, 1.0);
}
```

The fragment shader (texture.frag) will work as-is. There is one more task, however; we need to get the *MVPMatrix*'s location so that we can set it later. Put the following code in main() underneath the code that binds *texSampler* to unit *0* (look for *texSamplerUniformLoc*):

```
    // Get other uniform locations
    GLint mvpMatrixLoc = glGetUniformLocation(shaderProg, "mvpMatrix");
    if (mvpMatrixLoc < 0) {
```

```
        SDL_Log("ERROR: Couldn't get mvpMatrix's location.");
        return EXIT_FAILURE;
    }
```

Building the 3D Cube

The *Vertex* structure also needs a 3D position to match the *vertPos* in the updated shader. So do that now:

```
/** Encapsulates the data for a single vertex.
 * Must match the vertex shader's input.
 */
typedef struct Vertex_s {
    float position[3];
    float texCoord[2];
} Vertex;
```

NOTE: The position parameter is now an array of length *3* instead of 2.

OpenGL also needs to know about the new vertex position size, so find the *glVertexAttribPointer()* call for *positionIdx*, and update it to be a 3D vector:

```
    glVertexAttribPointer(positionIdx, 3, GL_FLOAT, GL_FALSE,
        sizeof(Vertex), (const GLvoid*)0);
```

NOTE: The one change is that the second parameter is now a *3*.

We're going to render a cube, so the *vertices* array needs to be updated. Here's where things get a little more complicated. Last time we rendered a triangle-fan/quad. Now we're going to render a 3D cube with multiple sides. This will be done with triangles.

We could store every triangle in the vertex array separately, but that would mean a lot of duplicate vertices (each vertex is used by 6 triangles). OpenGL allows us to avoid such duplication by using an index array. More about that later. First, here's the big array of vertices:

```
    // Create the 3D cube
    float cubeSize_2 = 100.0f / 2.0f; // Half the cube's size
    const Vertex vertices[] = {
        // Front face
        {{-cubeSize_2, -cubeSize_2,  cubeSize_2},{0.0f, 0.0f}},
```

```
    {{ cubeSize_2, -cubeSize_2,  cubeSize_2},{1.0f, 0.0f}},
    {{ cubeSize_2,  cubeSize_2,  cubeSize_2},{1.0f, 1.0f}},
    {{-cubeSize_2,  cubeSize_2,  cubeSize_2},{0.0f, 1.0f}},
    // Back face
    {{ cubeSize_2, -cubeSize_2, -cubeSize_2},{0.0f, 0.0f}},
    {{-cubeSize_2, -cubeSize_2, -cubeSize_2},{1.0f, 0.0f}},
    {{-cubeSize_2,  cubeSize_2, -cubeSize_2},{1.0f, 1.0f}},
    {{cubeSize_2,   cubeSize_2, -cubeSize_2},{0.0f, 1.0f}},
    // Left face
    {{-cubeSize_2, -cubeSize_2, -cubeSize_2},{0.0f, 0.0f}},
    {{-cubeSize_2, -cubeSize_2,  cubeSize_2},{1.0f, 0.0f}},
    {{-cubeSize_2,  cubeSize_2,  cubeSize_2},{1.0f, 1.0f}},
    {{-cubeSize_2,  cubeSize_2, -cubeSize_2},{0.0f, 1.0f}},
    // Right face
    {{ cubeSize_2, -cubeSize_2,  cubeSize_2},{0.0f, 0.0f}},
    {{ cubeSize_2, -cubeSize_2, -cubeSize_2},{1.0f, 0.0f}},
    {{ cubeSize_2,  cubeSize_2, -cubeSize_2},{1.0f, 1.0f}},
    {{ cubeSize_2,  cubeSize_2,  cubeSize_2},{0.0f, 1.0f}},
    // Top face
    {{ cubeSize_2,  cubeSize_2, -cubeSize_2},{0.0f, 0.0f}},
    {{-cubeSize_2,  cubeSize_2, -cubeSize_2},{1.0f, 0.0f}},
    {{-cubeSize_2,  cubeSize_2,  cubeSize_2},{1.0f, 1.0f}},
    {{ cubeSize_2,  cubeSize_2,  cubeSize_2},{0.0f, 1.0f}},
    // Bottom face
    {{-cubeSize_2, -cubeSize_2, -cubeSize_2},{0.0f, 0.0f}},
    {{ cubeSize_2, -cubeSize_2, -cubeSize_2},{1.0f, 0.0f}},
    {{ cubeSize_2, -cubeSize_2,  cubeSize_2},{1.0f, 1.0f}},
    {{-cubeSize_2, -cubeSize_2,  cubeSize_2},{0.0f, 1.0f }}};
```

Each vertex in the array above has a number (i.e., its index), starting at 0 for the first one. The index array is used to select which vertices to draw. For example, array {0, 1, 2} would draw a triangle using the first three vertices. The array {0, 1, 2, 2, 3, 0} would draw two triangles using vertices 0 to 3, which is the cube's front face.[3]

The cube's index array is easily generated with a loop:

---

3   See the "Index Array" section of the Modern Graphics Programming Primer for more: https://keasigmadelta.com/graphics-primer

```cpp
    // Generate the index array
    const GLsizei vertsPerSide = 4;
    const GLsizei numSides = 6;
    const GLsizei indicesPerSide = 6;
    const GLsizei numIndices = indicesPerSide * numSides;
    GLushort indices[numIndices];
    GLuint i = 0;
    for (GLushort j = 0; j < numSides; ++j) {
        GLushort sideBaseIdx = j * vertsPerSide;
        indices[i++] = sideBaseIdx + 0;
        indices[i++] = sideBaseIdx + 1;
        indices[i++] = sideBaseIdx + 2;
        indices[i++] = sideBaseIdx + 2;
        indices[i++] = sideBaseIdx + 3;
        indices[i++] = sideBaseIdx + 0;
    }
```

IMPORTANT: Use *GLushort* for index arrays instead of *GLuint*, because OpenGL ES doesn't guarantee that *GL_UNSIGNED_INT* is supported. Using *GLushort* is also more compact (it's 16-bits per index instead of 32).

Similarly to vertices, indices are best stored in an Index Buffer Object (IBO). So, add two new functions to *Main.cpp* (above *main()*) for that task:

```cpp
/** Creates the Index Buffer Object (IBO) containing
 * the given indices.
 *
 * @param indices pointer to the array of indices
 * @param numIndices the number of indices in the array
 */
GLuint iboCreate(GLushort *indices, GLuint numIndices) {
    // Create the Index Buffer Object
    GLuint ibo;
    int nBuffers = 1;
    glGenBuffers(nBuffers, &ibo);
    glBindBuffer(GL_ELEMENT_ARRAY_BUFFER, ibo);

    // Copy the index data in, and deactivate
```

```c
    glBufferData(GL_ELEMENT_ARRAY_BUFFER, sizeof(indices[0]) * numIndices,
indices,
        GL_STATIC_DRAW);
    glBindBuffer(GL_ELEMENT_ARRAY_BUFFER, 0);

    // Check for problems
    GLenum err = glGetError();
    if (err != GL_NO_ERROR) {
        // Failed
        glDeleteBuffers(nBuffers, &ibo);
        SDL_Log("Creating IBO failed, code %u\n", err);
        ibo = 0;
    }

    return ibo;
}

/** Frees the IBO.
 *
 * @param vbo the IBO's name.
 */
void iboFree(GLuint ibo) {
    glDeleteBuffers(1, &ibo);
}
```

Now call *iboCreate()* from main, just below the index generation code:

```c
    GLuint ibo = iboCreate(indices, numIndices);
    if (!ibo) {
        // Failed. Error message has already been printed, so just quit
        return EXIT_FAILURE;
    }
```

Like the VBO, the IBO also needs to be bound before use:

```c
    // Bind the index array for use
    glBindBuffer(GL_ELEMENT_ARRAY_BUFFER, ibo);
```

GlDrawElements() will now read indices from *ibo*.

For completeness, call *iboDestroy()* in the cleanup section at the end of *main()*:

```
    iboFree(ibo);
    ibo = 0;
```

Simulating the Virtual World

Okay, so the shaders are set up and we have a 3D model ready to go. Now we need to build the virtual world. It's a simple 3D scene: a camera pointed at a single cube.

As explained earlier, objects and cameras are modelled using matrices. To build those matrices, start by including the headers of GLM (our matrix/vector algebra library of choice) in *Main.cpp*:

```
#include <glm/glm.hpp>
#include <glm/gtc/matrix_transform.hpp>
#include <glm/gtc/type_ptr.hpp>
```

Now scroll down to just above the *glDrawArrays()* call in *main()*. Insert the following code to set the cube's pose:[4]

```
    // Set the object's pose
    glm::mat4 modelMat = glm::rotate(glm::mat4(1.0f), (float)M_PI / 4,
glm::vec3(1.0f, 0.0f, 0.0f));
    modelMat = glm::rotate(modelMat, (float)M_PI / 4, glm::vec3(0.0f, 1.0f,
0.0f));
```

The cube is located at the world origin (coordinate: *(0, 0, 0)*), but has been rotated along the x and y axes so that the camera gets an interesting view.

Next up, the camera. The camera has two matrices; one for its pose in the world (the view matrix), and a projection matrix that models the camera's optics. Here's the code to position the camera so it can see the cube:

```
    // Set up the camera
    // NOTE: OpenGL cameras look down the negative z-axis
    float camPosX = 0.0f;
    float camPosY = 0.0f;
    float camPosZ = 150.0f;
    glm::mat4 viewMat = glm::translate(glm::mat4(1.0f),
        glm::vec3(-camPosX, -camPosY, -camPosZ));
```

---

4   An object's pose is its position and orientation.

OpenGL cameras look down their negative z-axis, so the easiest way to see the cube is to move it in the opposite direction. Notice how *viewMatrix* translation is negative. This is because the view matrix transforms *from* world coordinates instead of the other way round.

GLM has a convenient function to generate the projection matrix called *perspective()*. Let's create a camera with a 60° viewing angle lens:

```
glm::mat4 projMat = glm::perspective(glm::radians(60.0f),
    (float)DISP_WIDTH / (float)DISP_HEIGHT, 1.0f, 1000.f);
```

These three matrices now need to be combined into the Model-View-Projection (MVP) matrix, and passed on to the vertex shader. This is a simple multiplication and uniform upload operation:

```
// Upload the shader uniforms
glm::mat4 mvpMat = projMat * viewMat * modelMat;
glUniformMatrix4fv(mvpMatrixLoc, 1, GL_FALSE, glm::value_ptr(mvpMat));
```

Drawing

Everything is set up, so we can finally draw the cube! Replace the *glDrawArray()* call with the following:

```
// Now draw!
glDrawElements(GL_TRIANGLES, numIndices, GL_UNSIGNED_SHORT, (GLvoid*)0);
```

Save the file, compile the program and run it. Oh dear, that doesn't look quite right now does it (Figure 12)? We must have forgotten something...

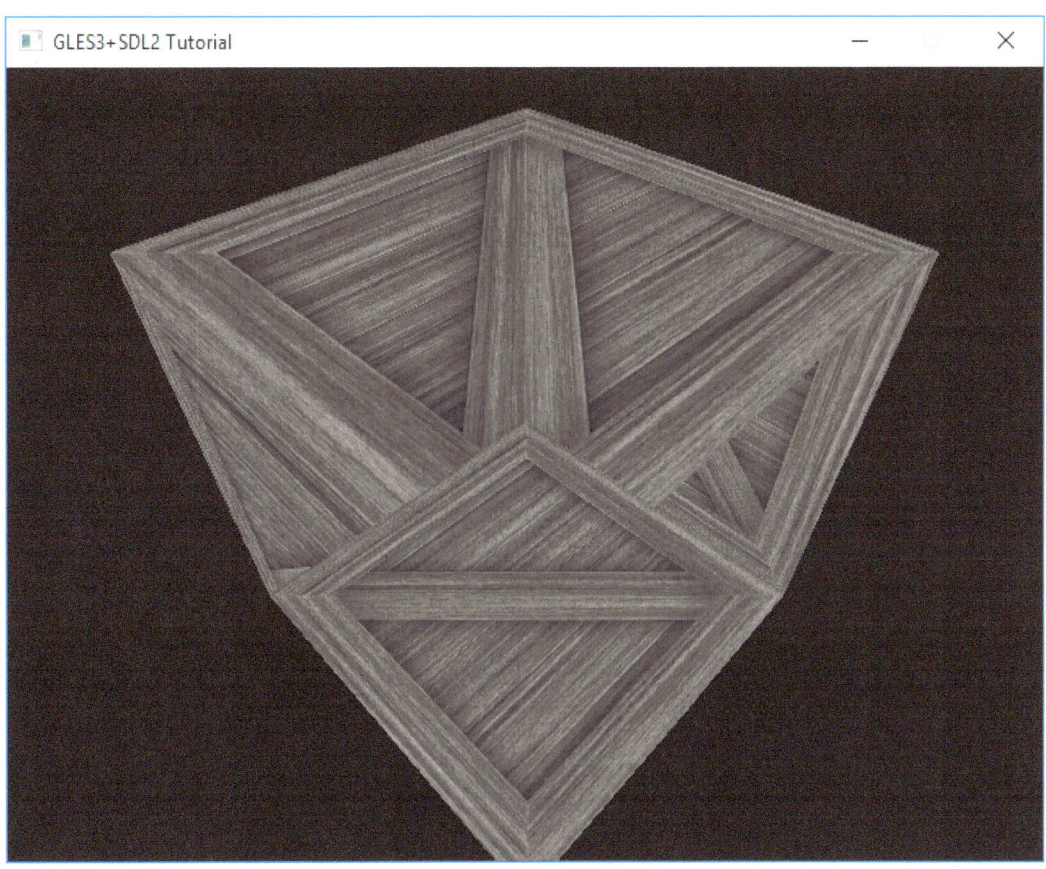

Figure 12: The rendered 3D box doesn't look right because the floor ended up on top.

The Depth Buffer

The reason why the image looks wrong, is because the cube's floor is rendered last, and no check is made whether or not it's actually visible. Physically, the cube's floor is hidden from view by the other faces that are closer to the camera.

The GPU needs to check if something closer has already been rendered or not, and that's where the depth-buffer comes in. The depth-buffer stores the distance from the camera to whatever has been rendered for each pixel. When something new is rendered, its distance is compared to what has been rendered before, and only objects that are closer are drawn.[5]

So, how is the depth buffer set up? Insert the following code above the *glClear()* call:

```
// Enable and set up the depth buffer
glEnable(GL_DEPTH_TEST);
glDepthFunc(GL_LESS);
```

This enables the depth buffer (which already exists), and sets the depth comparison function to check if the depth is *less* than what's already been rendered.

The depth buffer also needs to be cleared or old garbage could create holes in our image. A depth buffer value of *1.0* indicates infinitely far away, so that's what we'll set it to. Replace the original *glClear()* code with the following:

```
// Clear to black
glClearColor(0.0f, 0.0f, 0.0f, 1.0f);
glClearDepthf(1.0f);
glClear(GL_COLOR_BUFFER_BIT | GL_DEPTH_BUFFER_BIT);
```

Now compile and run the code. With the depth buffer is set up we finally get the 3D scene we want (Figure 13). It looks a little flat, though. That's because there are no lighting calculations. We'll fix this in the next tutorial...

---

5   See the "Depth Buffer" section of the Modern Graphics Programming Primer for more:
     https://keasigmadelta.com/graphics-primer

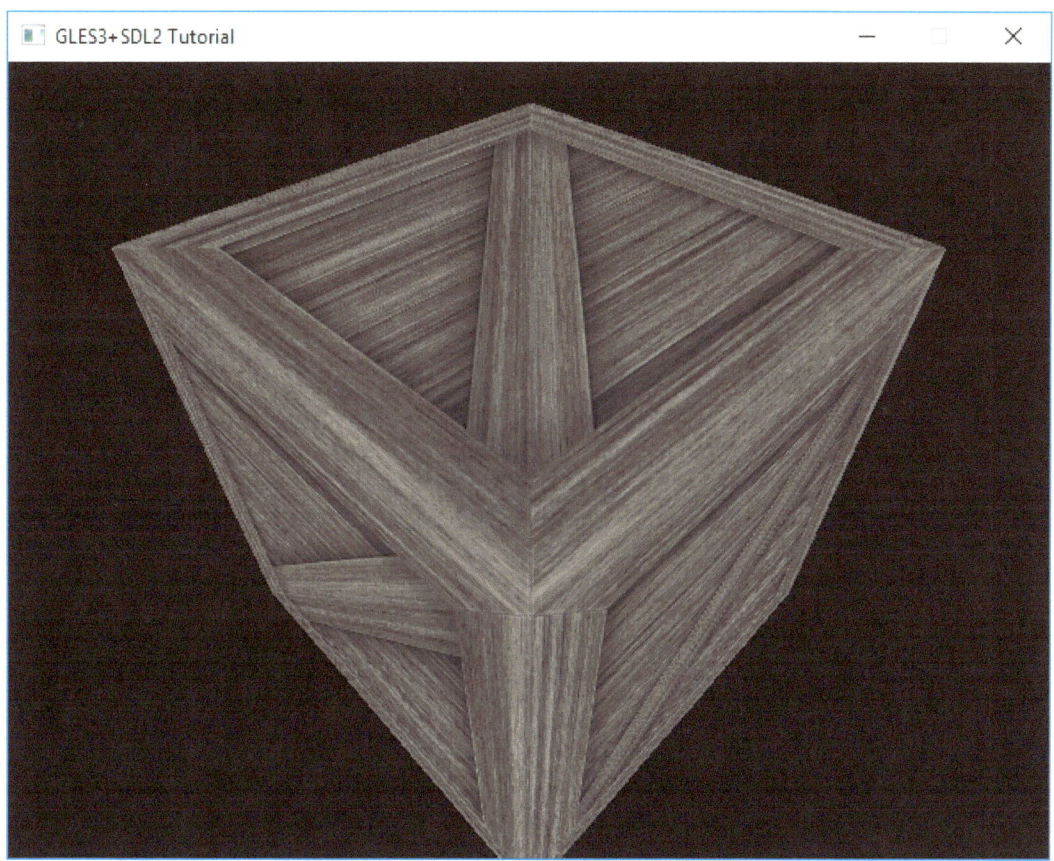

Figure 13: The texture-mapped wooden box looking the way it ought.

Exercises

1. Change the box's orientation so you see it from a different angle

2. Move the camera to a different position

3. Change the camera lens' viewing angle to zoom in or out

   HINT: You may have to move the camera too to compensate

4. Render two cubes with different poses

   HINT: The second cube has its own model matrix, resulting in a new MVP matrix

Tutorial 5: Lighting

The previous tutorial's rendered image looks a little flat and lifeless (Figure 13). The real world has lights and shadows, and that's what's missing. So let's add a light to our virtual world.

We're going to add a single point light source. There are other light types (e.g., spotlights), but lets stick to the simplest one for now.

Theory

Try this: switch on a desk lamp and hold a ball under it. Notice how the object is bright where the lamp is shining on it, and in shadow on the opposite side. You might be thinking, "well duh, of course it's like that." Bear with me for a moment.

Look more closely at the ball. Notice how the ball is brightest where its surface is facing the lamp directly, and becomes darker as the surface's angle shifts away from the lamp. It's finally in shadow where the surface is perpendicular (90°) to the lamp.

Our lighting calculations need to simulate this effect. We're going to use a simple diffuse colour model. It misses things such as shiny reflections, but it's important to keep things simple. For more about lighting, have a look in the "Modern Graphics Programmer Primer's" Lighting section.[6]

IMPORTANT: 3D lighting calculations involve vector algebra. If you have difficulty with the mathematics, then focus on the concepts behind them.

Diffuse Lighting

Surfaces with microscopic roughness tend to reflect light that hits it in all directions. This is called diffuse diffuse reflection.

As observed earlier, the brightness of that reflection depends on the angle between the surface and the oncoming light. To calculate the brightness, we need to know the direction the surface is facing (known as the *surface normal* **n**), and the direction to the light (**l**). This is shown in Figure 14.

---

6   https://keasigmadelta.com/graphics-primer

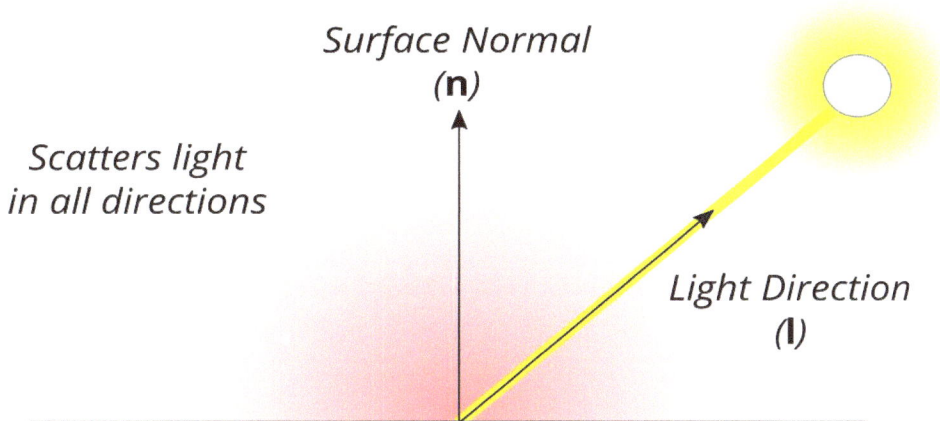

Figure 14: Diffuse lighting depends on the surface normal and light direction.

Mathematically, this is given by the following formula:

$\mathbf{i_d} = max(k_d \mathbf{i}(\mathbf{n} \cdot \mathbf{l}), 0)$

k_d is the diffuse reflection constant, and $\mathbf{i_d}$ is the reflected light intensity, and $(\mathbf{n} \cdot \mathbf{l})$ is the dot-product of the surface normal and light direction. The dot-product $(\mathbf{n} \cdot \mathbf{l})$ is what models the reflected brightness dropping to *0* as the angle between the surface normal and light vectors increases.

The *max()* function is used to prevent the brightness from going negative when the surface faces away from the light. There's no such thing as negative light.

Ambient Light

The diffuse reflection formula above works well, but the side in shadow ends up being pitch black. This is uncommon in the real world because light can bounce many times from one object to another creating a sort of directionless background light (a.k.a., ambient light).

It's theoretically possible to simulate this light using techniques such as raytracing. However, it's very computationally intensive, so we're going to use a simple approximation. And I mean, really simple.

We're going to pretend that ambient light is a single constant. Real ambient light is much more complicated, but using a constant is really easy and gives surprisingly decent results (a lot of the time). Here's the mathematical formula:

$$\mathbf{i_a} = k_a\mathbf{i}$$

k_a is the ambient reflection constant, and $\mathbf{i_a}$ is the reflected ambient light intensity.

Putting it All Together

To get the final surface colour, we simply add the diffuse and ambient contributions together:

$$\mathbf{i_s} = max(k_d\mathbf{i}(\mathbf{n{\cdot}l}),\ 0) + k_a\mathbf{i}$$

$\mathbf{i_s}$ is the surface colour, as viewed by the eye/camera. Multiple lights can be handled simply by adding the diffuse, and ambient reflections from all lights together.

Getting Started

Phew, that was a lot of theory. Time to put it into practise. As with previous tutorials, create a new project (GLTutorial5), copy the files from the previous tutorial, and add them to the project.

With Visual Studio you'll also have to install SDL_image and GLM again. Do this by entering the following in the NuGet Package Manager Console:

```
Install-Package sdl2_image.v140
```

```
Install-Package GLMathematics
```

Remember to also add the GLM include directory to the "Include Directories" the same way you did it last tutorial. For convenience, here's the full include directories line I ended up with:

```
angle\include;..\packages\GLMathematics.0.9.5.4\build\native\include;$(IncludePath)
```

Shaders

The Vertex Shader

The vertex shader (texture.vert) needs some major additions. For starters, it needs to know the surface's normal. Theoretically this could be calculated from the triangle vertices, but it's much more efficient to precalculate them, and store them as a separate input:

```
layout(location = 2) in vec3 vertNormal;
```

The fragment shader needs a per-pixel copy of the surface normal and the light position vector:

```
out vec3 normal;
out vec3 lightVec;
```

There are also some new uniform variables. Firstly, the MVP matrix needs to be separated out. Next, normals need to be rotated by a special matrix, and the shader must know the light's position:

```
uniform mat4 mvMat;
uniform mat4 normalMat;
uniform mat4 projMat;
uniform vec3 lightPos; // NOTE: position in view space (so after
                       // (being transformed by its own MV matrix)
```

In *main()*, calculating the position becomes a two-step process:

```
    // Calc. the position in view space
    vec4 viewPos = mvMat * vec4(vertPos, 1.0);

    // Calc the position
    gl_Position = projMat * viewPos;
```

Next, the surface normal is transformed into view space:

```
  // Transform the normal

  normal = normalize((normalMat * vec4(vertNormal, 1.0)).xyz);
```

Finally, the light position is calculated relative to the current position (i.e., relative to *viewPos*) :

```
// Calc. the light vector
lightVec = lightPos - viewPos.xyz;
```

That's it for the vertex shader; the fragment shader takes over from here. For convenience, here's the full shader code:

```
#version 300 es

layout(location = 0) in vec3 vertPos;
layout(location = 1) in vec2 vertTexCoord;
layout(location = 2) in vec3 vertNormal;

out vec2 texCoord;
out vec3 normal;
out vec3 lightVec;

uniform mat4 mvMat;
uniform mat4 normalMat;
uniform mat4 projMat;
uniform vec3 lightPos; // NOTE: position in view space (so after
                       //       (being transformed by its own MV matrix)

void main() {
    // Pass on the texture coordinate
    texCoord = vertTexCoord;

    // Calc. the position in view space
    vec4 viewPos = mvMat * vec4(vertPos, 1.0);

    // Calc the position
    gl_Position = projMat * viewPos;

    // Transform the normal
    normal = normalize((normalMat * vec4(vertNormal, 1.0)).xyz);

    // Calc. the light vector
    lightVec = lightPos - viewPos.xyz;
}
```

The Fragment Shader

The fragment shader has two new inputs that match the vertex shader's new outputs:

```
in vec3 normal;
in vec3 lightVec;
```

It also needs two new uniforms for the diffuse colour ($k_d\mathbf{i}$), and ambient colour ($k_a\mathbf{i}$). These uniforms combine the light colour and material reflectivity constants into one for efficiency:

```
uniform vec3 ambientCol; // The light and object's combined ambient colour
uniform vec3 diffuseCol; // The light and object's combined diffuse colour
```

Ambient lighting is the easiest to calculate:

```
    // Base colour (from the diffuse texture)
    vec4 colour = texture(texSampler, texCoord);

    // Ambient lighting
    vec3 ambient = vec3(ambientCol * colour.xyz);
```

Diffuse lighting is a bit more complicated:

```
    // Calculate the light attenuation, and direction
    float distSq = dot(lightVec, lightVec);
    float attenuation = clamp(1.0 - invRadiusSq * sqrt(distSq), 0.0, 1.0);
    attenuation *= attenuation;
    vec3 lightDir = lightVec * inversesqrt(distSq);

    // Diffuse lighting
    vec3 diffuse = max(dot(lightDir, normal), 0.0) * diffuseCol * colour.xyz;
```

The light attenuation is how intense (bright) the light is, which reduces the farther away you are from the point light. I don't want to explain the attenuation formula in detail. It's designed to loosely approximate inverse square law,[7] bust also gives the light a maximum reach radius (given by *invRadiusSq*, which is *1/radius²*).

The final colour is calculated as follows:

```
// The final colour
// NOTE: Alpha channel shouldn't be affected by lights
vec3 finalColour = (ambient + diffuse) * attenuation;
fragColour = vec4(finalColour, colour.w);
```

Please compare the code carefully to the diffuse and ambient light formulae in the theory section. Make sure you can see how the code matches the formulae.

For convenience, here's the shader code in full:

```
#version 300 es

#ifdef GL_ES
precision highp float;
#endif

in vec2 texCoord;
in vec3 normal;
in vec3 lightVec;

out vec4 fragColour;

uniform sampler2D texSampler;
uniform vec3 ambientCol; // The light and object's combined ambient colour
uniform vec3 diffuseCol; // The light and object's combined diffuse colour

const float invRadiusSq = 0.00001;

void main() {
    // Base colour (from the diffuse texture)
    vec4 colour = texture(texSampler, texCoord);

    // Ambient lighting
```

---

7   A point light source's light intensity is given by the inverse square law: https://en.wikipedia.org/wiki/Inverse-square_law.

```glsl
    vec3 ambient = vec3(ambientCol * colour.xyz);

    // Calculate the light attenuation, and direction
    float distSq = dot(lightVec, lightVec);
    float attenuation = clamp(1.0 - invRadiusSq * sqrt(distSq), 0.0, 1.0);
    vec3 lightDir = lightVec * inversesqrt(distSq);

    // Diffuse lighting
    vec3 diffuse = max(dot(lightDir, normal), 0.0) * diffuseCol * colour.xyz;

    // The final colour
    // NOTE: Alpha channel shouldn't be affected by lights
    vec3 finalColour = (ambient + diffuse) * attenuation;
    fragColour = vec4(finalColour, colour.w);
}
```

Adding the Surface Normals

The vertex shader needs the surface normal at each vertex, so the *Vertex* structure needs to be updated again:

```c
/** Encapsulates the data for a single vertex.
 * Must match the vertex shader's input.
 */
typedef struct Vertex_s {
    float position[3];
    float texCoord[2];
    float normal[3];
} Vertex;
```

Now tell OpenGL where to find the *normal* vertex attribute. Add the following code below similar code for the position and texture coordinate (search for *glVertexAttribPointer()*):

```c
    GLuint normalIdx = 2;  // Normal is vertex attribute 2
    glVertexAttribPointer(normalIdx, 3, GL_FLOAT, GL_FALSE,
        sizeof(Vertex), (const GLvoid*)offsetof(Vertex, normal));
    glEnableVertexAttribArray(normalIdx);
```

Finally, the surface normals need to be added to the cube. Here's the new vertices array:

```cpp
const Vertex vertices[] = {
    // Front face
    {{-cubeSize_2, -cubeSize_2,  cubeSize_2},{0.0f, 0.0f},
        {0.0f, 0.0f, 1.0f}},
    {{ cubeSize_2, -cubeSize_2,  cubeSize_2},{1.0f, 0.0f},
        {0.0f, 0.0f, 1.0f}},
    {{ cubeSize_2,  cubeSize_2,  cubeSize_2},{1.0f, 1.0f},
        {0.0f, 0.0f, 1.0f}},
    {{-cubeSize_2,  cubeSize_2,  cubeSize_2},{0.0f, 1.0f},
        {0.0f, 0.0f, 1.0f}},
    // Back face
    {{ cubeSize_2, -cubeSize_2, -cubeSize_2},{0.0f, 0.0f},
        {0.0f, 0.0f, -1.0f}},
    {{-cubeSize_2, -cubeSize_2, -cubeSize_2},{1.0f, 0.0f},
        {0.0f, 0.0f, -1.0f}},
    {{-cubeSize_2,  cubeSize_2, -cubeSize_2},{1.0f, 1.0f},
        {0.0f, 0.0f, -1.0f}},
    {{ cubeSize_2,  cubeSize_2, -cubeSize_2},{0.0f, 1.0f},
        {0.0f, 0.0f, -1.0f}},
    // Left face
    {{-cubeSize_2, -cubeSize_2, -cubeSize_2},{0.0f, 0.0f},
        {-1.0f, 0.0f, 0.0f}},
    {{-cubeSize_2, -cubeSize_2, cubeSize_2},{1.0f, 0.0f},
        {-1.0f, 0.0f, 0.0f}},
    {{-cubeSize_2,  cubeSize_2,  cubeSize_2},{1.0f, 1.0f},
        {-1.0f, 0.0f, 0.0f}},
    {{-cubeSize_2,  cubeSize_2, -cubeSize_2},{0.0f, 1.0f},
        {-1.0f, 0.0f, 0.0f}},
    // Right face
    {{ cubeSize_2, -cubeSize_2,  cubeSize_2},{0.0f, 0.0f},
        {1.0f, 0.0f, 0.0f}},
    {{ cubeSize_2, -cubeSize_2, -cubeSize_2},{1.0f, 0.0f},
        {1.0f, 0.0f, 0.0f}},
    {{ cubeSize_2,  cubeSize_2, -cubeSize_2},{1.0f, 1.0f},
        {1.0f, 0.0f, 0.0f}},
    {{ cubeSize_2,  cubeSize_2,  cubeSize_2},{0.0f, 1.0f},
        {1.0f, 0.0f, 0.0f}},
    // Top face
    {{ cubeSize_2,  cubeSize_2, -cubeSize_2},{0.0f, 0.0f},
        {0.0f, 1.0f, 0.0f}},
```

```
    {{-cubeSize_2, cubeSize_2, -cubeSize_2},{1.0f, 0.0f},
        {0.0f, 1.0f, 0.0f}},
    {{-cubeSize_2, cubeSize_2,  cubeSize_2},{1.0f, 1.0f},
        {0.0f, 1.0f, 0.0f}},
    {{ cubeSize_2, cubeSize_2,  cubeSize_2},{0.0f, 1.0f},
        {0.0f, 1.0f, 0.0f}},
    // Bottom face
    {{-cubeSize_2, -cubeSize_2, -cubeSize_2},{0.0f, 0.0f},
        {0.0f, -1.0f, 0.0f}},
    {{ cubeSize_2, -cubeSize_2, -cubeSize_2},{1.0f, 0.0f},
        {0.0f, -1.0f, 0.0f}},
    {{ cubeSize_2, -cubeSize_2,  cubeSize_2},{1.0f, 1.0f},
        {0.0f, -1.0f, 0.0f}},
    {{-cubeSize_2, -cubeSize_2,  cubeSize_2},{0.0f, 1.0f},
        {0.0f, -1.0f, 0.0f }}};
```

The index array (*indices*) remains unchanged.

Generating the New Uniform Variables

Both shaders have new uniform variables that must be calculated and uploaded. One of them (*normalMat*) is the inverse-transpose of the Model-View (MV) matrix. We need to include another header file to be able to calculate that, so put the following up the top of *Main.cpp*:

```
#include <glm/gtc/matrix_inverse.hpp>
```

Next, we need to get the new uniform's locations. So scroll down into *main()* and find the code that got the *mvpMatrix* uniform location, and replace it with the following:

```
// Get other uniform locations
GLint mvMatLoc = glGetUniformLocation(shaderProg, "mvMat");
if (mvMatLo
        c < 0) {
    SDL_Log("ERROR: Couldn't get mvMat's location.");
    return EXIT_FAILURE;
}
GLint normalMatLoc = glGetUniformLocation(shaderProg, "normalMat");
if (normalMatLoc < 0) {
    SDL_Log("ERROR: Couldn't get normalMat's location.");
    return EXIT_FAILURE;
```

```cpp
    }
    GLint projMatLoc = glGetUniformLocation(shaderProg, "projMat");
    if (projMatLoc < 0) {
        SDL_Log("ERROR: Couldn't get projMat's location.");
        return EXIT_FAILURE;
    }
    GLint lightPosLoc = glGetUniformLocation(shaderProg, "lightPos");
    if (lightPosLoc < 0) {
        SDL_Log("ERROR: Couldn't get lightPos's location.");
        return EXIT_FAILURE;
    }
    GLint ambientColLoc = glGetUniformLocation(shaderProg, "ambientCol");
    if (ambientColLoc < 0) {
        SDL_Log("ERROR: Couldn't get ambientCol's location.");
        return EXIT_FAILURE;
    }
    GLint diffuseColLoc = glGetUniformLocation(shaderProg, "diffuseCol");
    if (diffuseColLoc < 0) {
        SDL_Log("ERROR: Couldn't get diffuseCol's location.");
        return EXIT_FAILURE;
    }
```

With that in place, we can set up the lights and matrices. Here's the code that generates and uploads these uniforms:

```cpp
// Set up the light
// NOTE: AmbientCol and diffuseCol are the combined colour of both the
// light and the object's material properties
glm::vec3 lightPos(camPosX + 50.0f, camPosY + 80.0f, camPosZ);
glm::vec3 ambientCol(0.15f, 0.15f, 0.15f);
glm::vec3 diffuseCol(1.2f, 1.2f, 1.2f);


// Upload the shader uniforms
glm::mat4 mvMat = viewMat * modelMat;
glm::mat4 normalMat = glm::inverseTranspose(mvMat);
glUniformMatrix4fv(mvMatLoc, 1, GL_FALSE, glm::value_ptr(mvMat));
glUniformMatrix4fv(normalMatLoc, 1, GL_FALSE, glm::value_ptr(normalMat));
glUniformMatrix4fv(projMatLoc, 1, GL_FALSE, glm::value_ptr(projMat));
glUniform3fv(lightPosLoc, 1, glm::value_ptr(lightPos));
```

```
glUniform3fv(ambientColLoc, 1, glm::value_ptr(ambientCol));
glUniform3fv(diffuseColLoc, 1, glm::value_ptr(diffuseCol));
```

NOTE: Remember to delete *mvpMat* and related code; the shader doesn't use that any more.

Lights, Camera, & Action

Okay, that's all the code changes done. Compile and run it. If you did everything correctly, then you should be greeted with the image in Figure 15. Looks much better, eh?

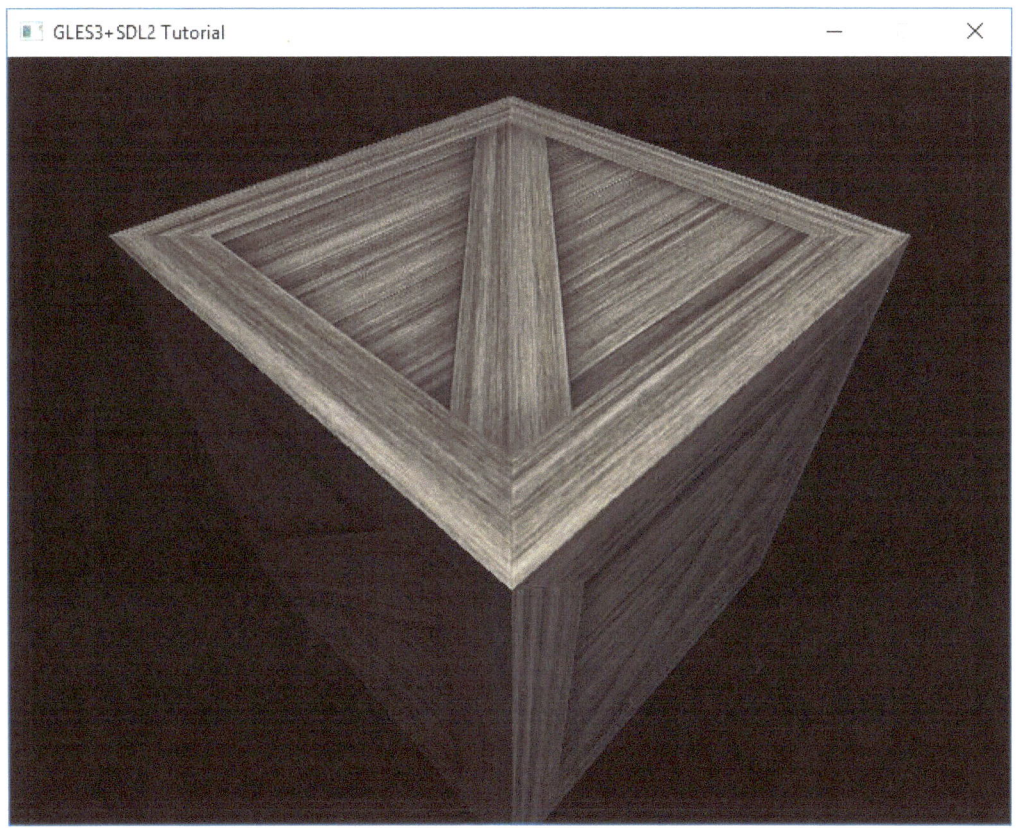

Figure 15: The wooden crate with one point light source (diffuse lighting model).

Exercises

1. Change the light's colour to red, or yellow

HINT: change *ambientCol* & *diffuseCol*

2. Move the light to a different position

3. Adjust the light's intensity

   HINT: change *ambientCol* & *diffuseCol*

4. Add a second light source

   HINT: You can turn *lightPos* and related uniforms into arrays (both the main code and shaders)

5. Have two lights with different colours

Tutorial 5a: Animation

Okay, one more tutorial because static images are rather boring. Let's liven things up, and animate the cube.

Getting Started

No need to create a new project, as this tutorial is an extension of the last one. Instead, add the following include to the top of *Main.cpp*:

```
#include <glm/gtx/transform.hpp>
```

It adds some extra transformation functions that are useful.

The Event Loop

Up till now all tutorials have rendered a single image and then waited for the user to quit via *SDL_WaitEvent()*. To animate the cube we need to regularly generate new frames (image) to display. So, we need to switch to a loop.

The new loop will:

- Check to user events (like the user clicking on the close button)

- Animate the cube (i.e., update the cube's pose)

- Draw the next frame

- Go back to the beginning

The first step is to replace *SDL_WaitEvent()* with *SDL_PollEvent()*:

```cpp
// Handle events
SDL_Event event;
if (SDL_PollEvent(&event) != 0) {
    if (event.type == SDL_QUIT) {
        // User wants to quit
        quit = true;
    }
}
```

SDL_PollEvent() also checks if an event has occurred, but will return immediately if there was no event. So our main loop now regularly checks (polls) for new events.

Next, shift rendering of the image into the polling loop. To do this, copy the *glClear()*, *glDrawElements()* and *SDL_GL_SwapWindow()* calls into the main loop:

```
// Redraw
glClear(GL_COLOR_BUFFER_BIT | GL_DEPTH_BUFFER_BIT);
glDrawElements(GL_TRIANGLES, numIndices, GL_UNSIGNED_SHORT,
    (GLvoid*)0);

// Update the window (flip the buffers)
SDL_GL_SwapWindow(window);
```

If you run the program now, then you'll see exactly the same cube. However, it'll be redrawn many times a second. You can't see that, though, because it's not animated yet.

Frame-Rate Independent Animation

The animation will be really simple; the cube will rotate at a constant rate. We want it to rotate at the same speed regardless of how fast or slow the machine is, or what else the computer is doing. So, time must be measured.

Add the following just above the main loop (so above *while(!quit)*):

```
// Prepare the animation
float cubeAngVel = 0.75f;// Radians/s
glm::vec3 cubeRotAxis(1.0f, 0.0f, 0.0f);
```

Next, add the following after the event checking code (so after the section starting with *SDL_PollEvent()*):

```
// Animate
Uint32 currTime = SDL_GetTicks();
float elapsedTime = (float)(currTime - prevTime) / 1000.0f;
prevTime = currTime; // Prepare for the next frame
```

SDL_GetTicks() gets the time since the SDL library was started in milliseconds. The code above calculates the *elapsedTime* in seconds since the last time this code was executed.

Now for the actual animation code. Insert the following code directly below the time measurement code you just added:

```
modelMat = glm::rotate(cubeAngVel * elapsedTime, cubeRotAxis) *
    modelMat;
mvMat = viewMat * modelMat;
normalMat = glm::inverseTranspose(mvMat);
glUniformMatrix4fv(mvMatLoc, 1, GL_FALSE, glm::value_ptr(mvMat));
glUniformMatrix4fv(normalMatLoc, 1, GL_FALSE,
glm::value_ptr(normalMat));
```

The code above rotates the model by *cubeAngVel* radians/s, then recalculates the MV and normal matrices and uploads them to the GPU.

The Full Main Loop Code

Here's the entire main loop with the changes made above:

```
// Prepare the animation
float cubeAngVel = 0.75f;// Radians/s
glm::vec3 cubeRotAxis(1.0f, 0.0f, 0.0f);

// The main loop
bool quit = false;
Uint32 prevTime = SDL_GetTicks();
while (!quit) {
    // Handle events
    SDL_Event event;
    if (SDL_PollEvent(&event) != 0) {
        if (event.type == SDL_QUIT) {
            // User wants to quit
            quit = true;
        }
    }

    // Animate
    Uint32 currTime = SDL_GetTicks();
    float elapsedTime = (float)(currTime - prevTime) / 1000.0f;
    prevTime = currTime; // Prepare for the next frame
```

```
        modelMat = glm::rotate(cubeAngVel * elapsedTime, cubeRotAxis) *
            modelMat;
        mvMat = viewMat * modelMat;
        normalMat = glm::inverseTranspose(mvMat);
        glUniformMatrix4fv(mvMatLoc, 1, GL_FALSE, glm::value_ptr(mvMat));
        glUniformMatrix4fv(normalMatLoc, 1, GL_FALSE,
            glm::value_ptr(normalMat));

        // Redraw
        glClear(GL_COLOR_BUFFER_BIT | GL_DEPTH_BUFFER_BIT);
        glDrawElements(GL_TRIANGLES, numIndices, GL_UNSIGNED_SHORT,
(GLvoid*)0);

        // Update the window (flip the buffers)
        SDL_GL_SwapWindow(window);
    }
```

Run the new code, and you'll see the animated cube rotating complete with realistic lighting (Figure 16). Congratulations! You just rendered your first animated scene.

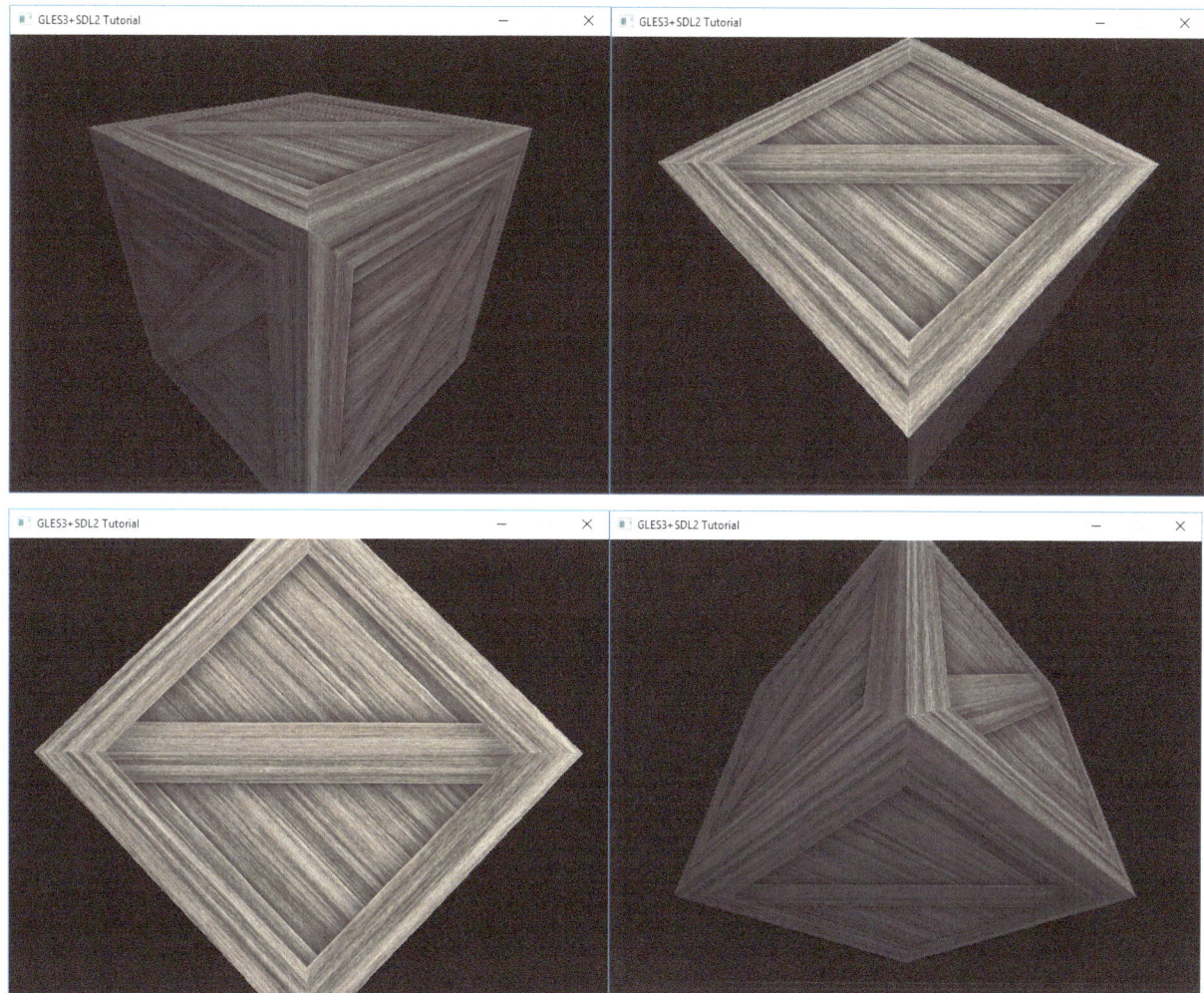

Figure 16: Four frames of the animated cube.

Exercises

Try to do the following:

1. Change the cube's rotation axis and speed

2. Make the cube's rotation axis change over time

3. Add another cube that rotates at a different speed

4. Make the camera orbit around the scene horizontally (so move the camera around the cube while continuing to face it)

5. Make the light orbit around the scene

What's Next

Congratulations on completing this tutorial! It's taken you from nothing to rendering a simple 3D scene. So, what to do next? Here are a few suggestions...

Updated Visual Studio Template

First up, here's a new Visual Studio template for you to use:

https://keasigmadelta.com/assets/GLTutorials/GLES3SDL2-Application-Extra.zip

This includes SDL2_image and GLM, so you don't have to set those up every time.

Learn More

There are plenty of OpenGL (ES) tutorials out there. I haven't found any ones for OpenGL ES 3+ that I'd recommend. The same goes for books. There are plenty of books out there, but they tend to be rather heavy. I have yet to make a shortlist. So for now, do your own search. If you find something great, then let me know.[8]

IMPORTANT: If you see any tutorials with *glBegin()/glEnd()*, then run away as fast as you can. The same goes for any tutorials using the old fixed pipeline (e.g., *glLight()*).

It's worth reading through the rest of the Modern Graphics Programming Primer.[9] In particular, you'll find the cheat-sheet and resources sections at the end to be quite handy.

Made Something Interesting/Awesome?

I'd love to hear from tutorial "graduates" who have made something interesting/awesome. So if that's you, then send me a message: https://keasigmadelta.com/about-us/contact-us/

---

8   https://keasigmadelta.com/about-us/contact-us/
9   https://keasigmadelta.com/graphics-primer